The Cato Institute

The Cato Institute is named for the libertarian pamphlets, *Cato's Letters,* which were inspired by the Roman Stoic, Cato the Younger. Written by John Trenchard and Thomas Gordon, *Cato's Letters* were widely read in the American colonies in the early eighteenth century and played a major role in laying the philosophical foundation for the revolution that followed. The erosion of civil and economic liberties in the modern world has occurred in concert with a widening array of social problems. These disturbing developments have resulted from a major failure to examine social problems in terms of the fundamental principles of human dignity, economic welfare, and justice.

The Cato Institute aims to broaden public policy debate by sponsoring programs designed to assist both the scholar and the concerned layperson in analyzing questions of political economy.

The programs of the Cato Institute include the sponsorship and publication of basic research in social philosophy and public policy; publication of major journals on the scholarship of liberty and commentary on political affairs; production of debate forums for radio; and organization of an extensive program of symposia, seminars, and conferences.

CATO INSTITUTE
747 Front Street
San Francisco, California 94111

A Theory of
Strict Liability

A Theory of
Strict Liability

Toward a Reformulation of Tort Law

Richard A. Epstein

With a Foreword by Mario Rizzo

CATO PAPER No. 8

INSTITUTE
San Francisco, California

Part One, "The Prima Facie Case in a Theory of Strict Lia-
bility," is reprinted from *The Journal of Legal Studies,* Vol.
II, No. 1, January 1973 (where it appeared under the title "A
Theory of Strict Liability"), with the permission of The
University of Chicago Law School.

Part Two, "Defenses and Subsequent Pleas in a Theory of
Strict Liability," is reprinted from *The Journal of Legal
Studies,* Vol. III, No. 1, January 1974 (where it appeared
under the title "Defenses and Subsequent Pleas in a System of
Strict Liability"), with the permission of The University of
Chicago Law School.

ISBN: 0-932790-08-9

Printed in the United States of America.

CATO INSTITUTE
747 Front Street
San Francisco, California 94111

CONTENTS

FOREWORD

Although Richard Epstein's theory of strict liability explains many aspects of contemporary tort law better than some more fashionable theories,[1] nevertheless it ought to be viewed as primarily normative in character. His version of strict liability is an attempt to base the prima facie case in a tort action solely on causal grounds. He then proceeds to develop some very straightforward causal and noncausal defenses to the valid prima facie case. In the development of his theory, Epstein emphasizes the ways in which it differs from a system of negligence, particularly the variety based on considerations of economic efficiency.

The negligence system of liability is not solely concerned with the relative equities between defendant and plaintiff but, to a great extent, with how their conduct measures up to some external standard. (As such, it is more nearly congruent with the spirit of criminal rather than tort law.[2]) Suppose, for example, that *A,* a driver, inadvertently hits *B,* a pedestrian, as *B* crosses the street. *A* will not be liable under a negligence system if he undertook "due care" to avoid the accident. However, even if *A* did not undertake due care, he might still escape liability if *B,* the victim, was himself contributorily negligent.[3] *B* might not have exercised the proper level of care to avoid being hit: Perhaps *B* could have been

---

[1]This is particularly true with respect to the fundamental principle underlying all of tort law: the tortfeasor takes his victim as he finds him. Similarly, negligence-sounding notions such as foreseeability are often thinly disguised veils for causal arguments. On this, see H. L. A. Hart and A. M. Honoré, Causation in the Law 230–60 (1959).

[2]See Richard A. Epstein, Crime and Tort: Old Wine in Old Bottles, in Assessing the Criminal: Restitution, Retribution and the Legal Process 231 (R. Barnett and J. Hagel III eds. 1977).

[3]Under a system of comparative negligence, however, contributory negligence of the plaintiff does not act as a *complete* bar to his recovery. Instead, it merely reduces his allowable recovery.

"reasonably" expected to wear brighter, more light-reflective clothes if he had crossed the street at night. Much of the inquiry in a negligence case, therefore, consists of a comparison between the levels of care actually undertaken by the parties and those that ought reasonably to have been undertaken.

Some of the more recent interpretations of negligence involve defining the due care standard in economic terms. However, this literature has not been clear or consistent in the meaning attached to an "economically efficient" level of care. In particular, some economists insist on a general equilibrium or socially optimum idea of nonnegligent behavior,[4] while others have retreated to a more narrow definition.[5] This narrower view consists of the attempted simulation of what the market would accomplish if there were zero transactions costs and if the parties were risk neutral.[6] Thus, for example, if the driver and the pedestrian could negotiate before the accident, the former *might* be willing to pay the latter more than enough to exercise due care. If this were indeed the case, then the market (or the narrowly construed efficient) solution might be simulated by placing liability on the plaintiff were he not to exercise due care. Parties who can make deals ex ante might prefer rules that minimize the sum of accident and accident-avoidance costs. In circumstances where such deals are infeasible, however, the law is viewed as an instrument of bringing about just that solution. How the courts might adequately determine what the market *would* do if it existed in a given area is a grave problem that, to my mind at least, has not been sufficiently analyzed.[7] Furthermore, the ethical justification for such attempted simulation of hypothetical markets cannot be easily defended.[8] The negligence/contributory-negligence system

[4]See generally Peter A. Diamond, Single Activity Accidents, 3 J. Leg. Studies 107 (1974).

[5]This appears to be the case in Richard A. Posner, Economic Analysis of Law (2d ed. 1977).

[6]This is the definition given in William M. Landes and Richard A. Posner, Negligence and Joint Torts: An Economic Analysis 1, n. 2 (unpublished, preliminary draft, 1979). For a critique applicable to both the general equilibrium and narrower conception of efficiency, see Mario J. Rizzo, Law Amid Flux: Negligence and Strict Liability in Tort, 9 J. Leg. Studies (forthcoming, 1980).

[7]This is discussed in Mario J. Rizzo, Uncertainty, Subjectivity and the Economic Analysis of Law, in Time, Uncertainty and Disequilibrium 84–86 (M. Rizzo ed. 1979).

[8]See the powerful critique in Ronald M. Dworkin, Is Wealth a Value?, 9 J. Leg. Studies (forthcoming, 1980).

implicitly embodies the peculiar position that a wrongful (negligent) act by the defendant imposes on the plaintiff an obligation to engage in certain acts or refrain from others in order to "earn" his right to recovery.

A system of strict liability, however, is preeminently based on causation. A is liable, at least prima facie, if he is the cause of B's harm, regardless of A's ability or inability to avoid the harm by the exercise of due care. Epstein does not undertake a detailed analysis of the notion of causation per se. This has been done admirably elsewhere.[9] Instead, he defines his causal ideas in terms of four simple common-sense paradigms.[10] They are (1) A hit B; (2) A frightened B; (3) A compelled B to hit C; and (4) A created a dangerous condition that resulted in harm to B. In a sense, these paradigms are conclusory: They presuppose an ability to recognize, on common sense principles, an instance of, say, A hit B. Therefore, the paradigms are more properly viewed as *classes* of causal relation.

The two most complex paradigms are clearly that of fear and dangerous condition. In the first case, extrasensitive plaintiffs may be thought to pose a potential problem.[11] Suppose that A wipes the sweat off his brow and then B falls dead of a heart attack.[12] This hypothetical properly raises two kinds of questions: one relating to causation and the other to damages. The fact that B "reacts" to A's conduct in such a drastic and unusual manner casts doubt on the existence of a causal relationship. Is this merely an instance of post hoc ergo propter hoc, or did A's act, for some strange reason, cause B to become terribly frightened? However, even if we assume the existence of a valid causal connection, the probability is arguably close to one that a purely innocent cause (e.g., the sound of thunder) would have frightened him to death in any event. Therefore, the expected present value of B's life just

---

[9]See Hart and Honoré, *supra,* note 1.

[10]This paradigmatic approach has been criticized in John Borgo, Causal Paradigms in Tort Law, 8 J. Leg. Studies 419 (1979). But see Richard A. Epstein, Causation and Corrective Justice: A Reply to Two Critics, 8 J. Leg. Studies, 478–87.

[11]See Borgo, *supra,* note 10 at 441–43.

[12]The manner in which both Epstein and Borgo state this hypothetical *presupposes* the causal relation. I prefer to start with a more neutral formulation. See Borgo, *supra,* note 10 at 441.

before *A* mopped his brow is very low.[13] Hence, the defendant, even if causally responsible, might well be liable for negligible or zero damages.

The paradigm of dangerous condition has wide applicability, especially in the area of products liability.[14] This paradigm makes clear at least one way in which Epstein's system of strict liability differs from what is fashionably referred to as strict products liability. Suppose a manufacturer produces a product that, when used as intended, explodes in the plaintiff's face. In Epstein's view the probability that such an explosion would occur is irrelevant: It may be very low, and yet prima facie liability would follow. All that is relevant is the causal connection *in this case.* Current strict products liability, on the other hand, requires demonstration that the product is "defective." Demonstration of the defective nature of that product involves a comparison of the probability and severity of the harm on the one side and the cost of "safety" on the other. Hence a product can explode in someone's face and yet not be defective if, ex ante, the costs exceed the benefits. Although the causal relation in the particular case may be clear, the plaintiff in a regime of "strict" products liability may not be able to establish even a valid prima facie case.

Until now we have dealt only with the prima facie case. As the second essay makes evident, Epstein's system includes both causal and noncausal defenses to the valid prima facie case. First, consider an example of a causal defense:

A hit *B* (valid prima facie case)

B compelled *A* to hit *B* (defense).

This is merely a use of one of the causal paradigms to shift the burden of responsibility back to the plaintiff. *A*'s act cannot be viewed as invasive since it was compelled by the "victim" himself. This is a complete causal defense. Other causal defenses, however, are only partial, as in the plea "*B* hit *A* to *B*'s own detriment." This is typical of accidents such as the collision of two automobiles. Partial defenses, naturally, lead to the apportionment of

---

[13]See generally Robert J. Peaslee, Multiple Causation and Damage, 47 Harv. L. Rev. 11–27 (1934).

[14]For Epstein's thoughts on this topic, see Richard A. Epstein, Products Liability: The Search for the Middle Ground, 56 N.C. L. Rev. 643 (1978).

liability, since there is causal responsibility on the part of both defendant and plaintiff.

The two major instances of *non*causal arguments in Epstein's system lie in the defenses of trespass and assumption of risk. Suppose, for example, that *A* created a dangerous condition on his land that resulted in harm to *B*. However, suppose further that *B* would not have been harmed were it not for his trespass on *A*'s land. *B* thus loses his right to recover against *A* because the harm of which *B* complains *arises out of* a wrongful invasion of the defendant's land. As Epstein says in Part Two, "The claims of exclusive possession would count for nothing if they did not serve as an independent ground to shift back to the plaintiff the risk of accidents that occurred on the defendant's land, when prima facie he had no business being there at all." The defense of assumption of risk admits of two variants: consensual agreement between plaintiff and defendant, and unilateral assumption by the plaintiff. Both completely bar the plaintiff's recovery because it can in no sense be claimed that the defendant has violated a right of the plaintiff when the latter *voluntarily* exposes himself to risk. To claim otherwise would deprive the plaintiff of the right to ex ante compensation for risk-taking. A system of corrective justice does not deprive an individual of the right to accept, for example, higher wages as compensation for higher-than-average risks on the job.

Although noncausal arguments play a role in a system of strict liability, the most important role, by far, must be given to the causal paradigms. The strong emphasis on causation is the major distinguishing factor between this theory of liability and its rivals. Yet it is important not to overestimate the general importance of causal principles. As Epstein himself has noted elsewhere,[15] the causal paradigms presuppose an allocation of ownership rights determined by noncausal principles. Conduct subsumed under these paradigms constitutes a violation of a logically prior property right. That *A* hit *B* is of no tortious consequence if *B* is an unowned physical entity. It is only because either *B* owns himself (self-ownership) or *B* is owned by *C* that a valid prima facie case for compensation can be established. In the former case, compensa-

[15]See Richard A. Epstein, Nuisance Law: Corrective Justice and Its Utilitarian Constraints, 8 J. Leg. Studies 50–53 (1979).

tion is owed *B*; and in the latter case, it is owed *C*. Although Epstein's paradigms are consistent with many different initial allocations of rights, they are not consistent with any notion of what "ownership" entails. For Epstein, violation of ownership rights is viewed largely in *physical* terms. Emitting sparks onto a farmer's crops can be actionable, but lowering the price of those crops by vigorous competition is not (at least under tort principles).

Recently, the economic-efficiency theorists have claimed that their view of tort law is preferable, in part because the same principles which determine tort liability in an economic framework can be used to allocate initial rights.[16] Hence no dichotomization of tort and rights theory is necessary. To be consistent with efficient resource allocation, the rule should be, "Distribute a right to the party who, in the absence of transactions costs, would have bought it." This allegedly ensures that the right will be given to whoever (on a social calculus) values it most. Space does not permit a detailed examination of this position here. Nevertheless, a few comments are in order. First, the essential principle underlying rights is that they must act as a trump or protection against distributions on the basis of the "general welfare."[17] Efficient resource allocation (or "wealth maximization" in the social sense) is no less an aggregative common-good idea than some of the vaguer notions fashionable in many quarters. Second, the casual mental experiments that decide the efficient allocation of a right are almost always *partial* equilibrium experiments. Suppose, for example, an individual has just bought (in a hypothetical market, of course) the right to his own labor. Will he have enough wealth remaining to be able to buy (if he so desired) the right to read pornography? The general equilibrium interconnection of rights "markets" is usually ignored because the problem is too difficult. Finally, to the extent that "society" is trying to allocate extremely basic or fundamental rights, significant wealth effects of a given initial distribution cannot be ignored. This is because the basic rights (e.g., to control one's own labor, to travel freely, etc.) presumably constitute a substantial proportion of an individual's full

---

[16]See Harold Demsetz, Wealth Distribution and the Ownership of Rights, 1 J. Leg. Studies 223 (1972) and, especially, Richard A. Posner, Utilitarianism, Economics and Legal Theory, 8 J. Leg. Studies 103 (1979).

[17]See generally Ronald M. Dworkin, Hard Cases, in Taking Rights Seriously 81 (1977).

wealth constraint. If this is the case, then the final allocation of rights will not be invariant with respect to the initial (and presumably arbitrary) distribution. This produces an insoluble problem. If the efficient allocation of rights is dependent on the initial (state-of-nature) distribution, then by what economic principle can this initial distribution be made? The answer, of course, is none, and thus the overstated claim of the efficiency hypothesis must collapse. Hence basic rights cannot be determined by reference to efficiency criteria, just as they cannot be determined by causal ideas.

Before concluding, explicit statement ought to be made of two major advantages that commend Epstein's system of strict liability. The first is based on the simple and appealing moral principle that he who causes harm should, at least prima facie, compensate the victim. Individual autonomy does not permit one individual to use another as a mere resource without compensation. The second is an economic advantage that I have discussed in detail elsewhere.[18] The greater simplicity of Epstein's system of strict liability in comparison with a negligence regime promotes what I have called "institutional efficiency." This is essentially the greater certainty that would be engendered in tort law—and consequently in the environment of economic agents—by the elimination of notions of "due care," "reasonableness," "negligence," etc. It is perhaps similar to the notion of economic or social coordination analyzed by the "Austrian" economists, particularly F. A. Hayek and Israel M. Kirzner.[19] The coordination of the activities of individuals rests heavily on the certainty imparted by the legal framework. In the restricted sense in which I am using the word, the coordination of activities need not correspond to an efficient allocation of resources. Efficiency in the conventional sense is neither a manageable nor moral goal for the legal system; it is time for justice and certainty to regain their central position.

September 1979   Mario J. Rizzo
                                               New York University

---

[18]See Rizzo, *supra,* note 6.

[19]See F. A. Hayek, The Use of Knowledge in Society, in Individualism and Economic Order 77 (1949) and Israel M. Kirzner, Competition and Entrepreneurship, 212–42 (1973).

PART ONE

The Prima Facie Case
in a
Theory of Strict Liability

I. Introduction

Torts is at once one of the simplest and one of the most complex
areas of the law. It is simple because it concerns itself with fact
patterns that can be understood and appreciated without the
benefit of formal legal instruction. Almost everyone has some
opinions, often strong even if unformed, about his rights and
responsibilities toward his fellow man; and almost everyone has
had occasion in contexts apart from the judicial process to apply
his beliefs to the question of responsibility for some mishap that
has come to pass. Indeed, the language of the law of tort, in sharp
contrast, say, to that of civil procedure, reveals at every turn its
origins in ordinary thought.

But the simplicity of torts based upon its use of ordinary language is deceptive. Even if ordinary language contains most of the
concepts that bear on questions of personal responsibility, it often
uses them in loose, inexact, and ambiguous ways: Witness, for
example, the confusion that surrounds the use of "malice." While
an intuitive appreciation of the persistent features of ordinary
language may help decide easy cases, more is required for the
solution of those difficult cases where the use of ordinary language pulls in different directions at the same time. There is need
for a systematic inquiry which refines, but which does not abandon,
the shared impressions of everyday life. The task is to develop a
normative theory of torts that takes into account common sense
notions of individual responsibility. Such a theory no doubt must
come to grips with the central concerns of the common law of

NOTE: I should like to thank Bruce A. Ackerman, Robert C. Ellickson, Thomas C.
Grey, and Hein D. Kötz for their valuable criticism and suggestions.—RAE

torts. But it need not (though it well may) embrace the common law solution to any particular problem.

This common sense approach to torts as a branch of common law stands in sharp opposition to much of the recent scholarship on the subject because it does not regard economic theory as the primary means to establish the rules of legal responsibility. A knowledge of the economic consequences of alternative legal arrangements can be of great importance, but even among those who analyze tort in economic terms there is acknowledgment of certain questions of "justice" or "fairness" rooted in common sense beliefs that cannot be explicated in terms of economic theory.[1] Even if they cannot provide satisfactory answers to fairness questions, the advocates of economic analysis in the law still insist that their work is of primary importance because it reduces the area in which fairness arguments must be judged in order to reach a decision in a particular case. But once it is admitted that there are questions of fairness as between the parties that are not answerable in economic terms, the exact role of economic argument in the solution of legal question becomes impossible to determine. It may well be that an acceptable theory of fairness can be reconciled with the dictates of economic theory in a manner that leaves ample room for the use of economic thought. But that judgment presupposes that some theory of fairness has been spelled out, which, once completed, may leave no room for economic considerations of any sort.

In order to raise these fairness questions in the context of traditional legal doctrine, I shall focus on the conflict that has persisted in the common law between theories of negligence and theories of strict liability. Chapter II argues that neither the moral nor economic accounts of negligence justify its dominance in the law of tort. Chapter III analyzes the different contexts in which it is appropriate to assert that "*A* caused *B* harm," and argues that this proposition, when properly understood, provides a suitable justification for the imposition of liability in tort. Chapter IV applies both the theories of negligence and of strict liability to the troublesome problem of the good Samaritan.

---

[1]See Guido Calabresi & A. Douglas Melamed, Property Rules, Liability Rules, and Inalienability: One View of the Cathedral, 85 Harv. L. Rev. 1089, 1102–05 (1972). But see Richard A. Posner, A Theory of Negligence, 1 J. Leg. Studies 29 (1972).

II. A Critique of Negligence

The development of the common law of tort has been marked by the opposition between two major theories. The first holds that a plaintiff should be entitled, prima facie, to recover from a defendant who has caused him harm only if the defendant intended to harm the plaintiff or failed to take reasonable steps to avoid inflicting the harm. The alternative theory, that of strict liability, holds the defendant prima facie liable for the harm caused whether or not either of the two further conditions relating to negligence and intent is satisfied.

It is most likely that theories of strict liability were dominant during the formative years of the common law. But during the nineteenth century, both in England and in this country, there was a decided and express shift toward the theories of negligence.[1] For the most part the impulses that supported the thrust toward a system of negligence liability were gounded on moral rather than on explicitly economic considerations. Indeed, the phrase "no liability without fault" was used to summarize the opposition to a system of strict liability on moral grounds.[2] At the turn of the century Ames

---

[1]The extent of the shift can be overstated; for Rylands v. Fletcher, L.R. 3 H.L. 330 (1868), was a case which, whatever its precise scope, accepted the principle of strict liability in at least some situations. The problem is that nowhere have the courts decided precisely where the principles of negligence should dominate and where they should not. For example, why should principles of strict liability dominate in products liability cases when automobile cases are decided, in general, in accordance with negligence principles? See Marc A. Franklin, Replacing the Negligence Lottery: Compensation and Selective Reimbursement, 53 Va. L. Rev. 774, 793 (1967). See also Harry Kalven, Jr., Torts: The Quest for Appropriate Standards, 53 Calif. L. Rev. 189, 205–06 (1965).

[2]Salmond, an influential writer at the turn of the century, often spoke of *"mens rea"* in the law of tort, even though he conceded that the term had a narrower meaning in the criminal law. See John Salmond, The Law of Torts 11 (7th ed. 1928).

described the transition from the early theories of strict liability to the modern theories of negligence in these confident terms:

> The early law asked simply, "Did the defendant do the physical act which damaged the plaintiff?" The law of today, except in certain cases based upon public policy, asks the further question, "Was the act blameworthy?" The ethical standard of reasonable conduct has replaced the unmoral standard of acting at one's peril.[3]

But the law of negligence never did conform in full to the requisites of the "moral" system of personal responsibility invoked in its behalf. In particular, the standard of the reasonable man, developed in order to ensure injured plaintiffs a fair measure of protection against their fellow citizens, could require a given person to make recompense even where no amount of effort could have enabled *him* to act in accordance with the standard of conduct imposed by the law. Certain defenses like insanity were never accepted as part of the law of negligence, even though an insane person is not regarded as morally responsible for his actions. But if Ames's original premise were correct, then it should follow from the "modern ethical doctrine" that a lunatic unable to appreciate the nature or consequences of his act ought not to be responsible for the damage he has inflicted upon another.[4]

Even if these exceptions to the general rule of negligence affect only a few of the cases to be decided, they do indicate a theoretical weakness that helps to explain efforts to find alternative justifications for the law of negligence couched in economic rather than moral terms. Thus, it was suggested that a defendant should be regarded as negligent if he did not take the precautions an economically prudent man would take in his own affairs, and, conversely, that where the defendant *did* conduct himself in an economically prudent manner, he could successfully defend himself in an action brought by another person whom he injured.

Although positions of this sort had been suggested from the beginning of this century,[5] they received their most famous expo-

---

[3] James Barr Ames, Law and Morals, 22 Harv. L. Rev. 97, 99 (1908).

[4] "[I]f insanity of a pronounced type exists, manifestly incapacitating the sufferer from complying with the rule which has been broken, good sense would require it to be admitted as an excuse." O. W. Holmes, Jr., The Common Law 109 (1881). See also James Barr Ames, *supra* note 3, at 99–100.

[5] See, *e.g.*, Henry T. Terry, Negligence, 29 Harv. L. Rev. 40 (1915).

sition in the opinion of Learned Hand in *United States v. Carroll Towing Co.*[6] The narrow point for decision in *Carroll Towing* was whether the *owner* of a barge owed to others a duty to keep a bargee or attendant on board while his barge was moored inside a harbor. In his analysis of the duty question, Hand notes that no general answer has been given to the question, and in his view for good reason:

> It becomes apparent why there can be no such general rule, when we consider the grounds for such a liability. Since there are occasions when every vessel will break from her moorings, and since, if she does, she becomes a menace to those about her . . . the owner's duty, as in other similar situations, to provide against resulting injuries is a function of three variables: (1) The probability that she will break away; (2) the gravity of the resulting injury, if she does; (3) the burden of adequate precautions.[7]

Hand expresses his conclusion in mathematical terms in order to demonstrate its applicability to the entire law of tort:

> if the probability be called P; the injury, L; and the burden, B; liability depends upon whether B is less than L multiplied by P: i.e., whether B [is less than] PL.[8]

Despite this implicitly economic ("cost-benefit") formulation of the concept of negligence, it does not appear that Hand in his analysis of the case has broken completely from the traditional view of negligence. True, he does note, consistent with the formula, that

> Applied to the situation at bar, the likelihood that a barge will break from her fasts and the damage she will do, vary with the place and time; for example, if a storm threatens, the danger is greater; so it is, if she is in a crowded harbor where moored barges are constantly being shifted about.[9]

But after these general observations, there is a marked shift in the style and logic of opinion, which suggests that after all he is more concerned with the traditional questions of "reasonableness" than with the systematic application of his economic formula:

[6]159 F. 2d 169 (2d Cir. 1947).

[7]*Id.* at 173.

[8]*Ibid.* The case for an economic interpretation of the Hand formula, as well as many of the subsidiary rules of negligence liability and damages, is argued in Richard A. Posner, *supra* chap. I, note 1.

[9]159 F.2d at 173.

> On the other hand, the barge must not be the bargee's prison, even though he lives aboard; he must go ashore at times. We need not say whether, even in such crowded waters as New York Harbor, a bargee must be aboard at night at all.[10]

The concern he expresses is unfounded. The duty imposed is a duty on the owner of the ship and not upon the bargee himself. There is no reason to assume that the owner could employ at most one bargee. The owner could have employed three bargees, each for eight hours, to protect the other ships in the harbor and still ensure that his barge would not be a prison for any of his employees.

But having limited himself to a rule requiring only one bargee, Hand proceeds to examine the conduct, not of the owner, but of the bargee and in the traditional manner so often used to decide the "reasonableness" of the defendant's conduct in negligence cases. The evidence showed that the bargee had been off the ship for a period in excess of twenty-one hours before the accident took place. Moreover, all he had to offer to explain his absence was some "fabricated" tale.[11] There was "no excuse for his absence," and it followed:

> In such circumstances we hold—and it is all that we do hold—that it was a fair requirement that the Conners Company should have a bargee aboard (unless he had some excuse for his absence), during the working hours of daylight.[12]

The use of the concept of "excuse" in Hand's formulation of the particular grounds for decision suggests that some of the elements material to determining "blameworthiness" in the moral sense are applicable with full force even after the statement of the general economic formula. But it is unclear what counts for Hand as an appropriate excuse within the framework of the law of tort. If the bargee left the ship in order to attend some emergency within the harbor, then presumably his absence would be "excused," but if so, no concept of excuse need be invoked. The formula itself covers this case because the defendant could show that the costs of prevention were high when measured against the alternative uses of the bargee's time.

Nor are other possible applications of the term clear. Suppose

[10]*Ibid.*
[11]*Id.* at 173–74.
[12]*Id.* at 174.

that the bargee was excused as a matter of contract because his employer allowed him to visit his family for the twenty-one-hour period of his absence. In these circumstances the bargee could no doubt plead the release as a valid excuse to any action brought by his employer on the contract. But it is doubtful whether the excuse of the bargee would be available to his employer in a separate action in tort brought against him by the injured party. If the employer released the bargee from his job for the day, presumably he would be under an obligation to hire a substitute, for the same reasons that he was under a duty to provide a bargee in the first instance. Finally, if the provision for "excuses" in Hand's opinion is designed to take into account good faith, insanity, mistake of fact and the like, then it serves to introduce into the back door the very problems that were confronted (even if not solved) by the theory of negligence based upon notions of personal blameworthiness. Thus, although Hand alludes to some non-economic concept of excuse, both its specific content and its relationship to the economic concept of negligence remain unclear.[13]

But even if the notion of "excuse" is put to one side, Hand's formula is still not free from difficulty. It is difficult to decide how to apply the formula when there is need for but a single precaution which one party is no better suited to take than the other. If, for example, there were two boats in a harbor, and need for but a single bargee, what result is appropriate if the two boats collide when both are unmanned? Is there negligence, or contributory negligence, or both? The formula is silent on the question of *which* ship should be manned. Yet that is the very question which must be answered, since in economic terms no bargee provides too little accident protection while two bargees provide too much.[14]

---

[13]Indeed, it is precisely the relationship between the economic tests for responsibility and the notion of excuse that troubles Calabresi in his recent article, because a theory of fairness is required to admit "excuses" into a system of liability rules. See Guido Calabresi & A. Douglas Melamed, *supra* chap. I, note 1, at 1102–05. Moreover, the need to take excuses into account explains why the concept of the "reasonable man" remains part of the law of negligence even after *Carroll Towing*.

[14]For a similar treatment of this same problem in the context of the English cases and the doctrine of reasonable foreseeability, see Abraham Harari, The Place of Negligence in the Law of Torts (1962). In particular, Harari argues that the law of negligence must develop some set of rules to *coordinate* the activities of several persons to decide which is under a duty to take precautions when each of them as a prudent man could reasonably foresee the prospect of danger. *Id.* at 105–24. See chap. IV, *infra,* for a discussion of affirmative duties in the law of tort.

These criticisms of the *Carroll Towing* formula are not limited to the special case where the parties find themselves, *ex ante,* in identical positions. Even if that assumption is relaxed, the same problems of coordination raised above stand in the way of the successful judicial application of the formula. It may be worthwhile for the owner of Ship *X* to take a given precaution only if the owner of Ship *Y* takes some particular, although different, precaution of his own. Thus, it could be that the use of a bargee on Ship *X* is indicated only if the owner of Ship *Y* installs warning lights on his ship, which would permit the bargee to respond in time to prevent the collision between the boats. In cases like this it is clear that the *Carroll Towing* formula must be revised to take into account not only the activities of the defendant but also those of the plaintiff. Indeed the problems of coordination are even more acute in those frequent cases where the appropriate pattern of cost minimization would require third persons not involved in the collision to take steps to prevent the harm in question. It is true that these difficulties do not render the *Carroll Towing* formula theoretically incoherent, but they do suggest that there may well be, despite its apparent simplicity, acute difficulties in its application. But we need not labor the point, for Learned Hand himself stated it well only two years after *Carroll Towing* was decided.

> It is indeed possible to state an equation for negligence in the form, $C = P \times D$, in which the C is the care required to avoid risk, D, the possible injuries, and P, the probability that the injuries will occur, if the requisite care is not taken. But of these factors care is the only one ever susceptible of quantitative estimate, and often that is not. The injuries are always a variable within limits, which do not admit of even approximate ascertainment; and, although probability might theoretically be estimated, if any statistics were available, they never are; and, besides, probability varies with the severity of the injuries. It follows that all such attempts are illusory, and, if serviceable at all, are so only to center attention upon which one of the factors may be determinative in any given situation.[15]

But even if the difficulties of application are put to one side, there are still further reasons why *both* the economic and moral views of negligence provide unsatisfactory bases for the law of tort. Both theories of negligence, for all their purported differences, share the common premise that once conduct is described

[15]Moisan v. Loftus, 178 F.2d 148, 149 (2d Cir. 1949).

as reasonable, no legal sanction ought to attach to it. In any system of common law liability, a court must allocate, explicitly or implicitly, a loss that has already occurred between the parties—usually two—before it. It could turn out that neither of the parties acted in a manner that was unreasonable or improper from either an economic or a moral point of view, but a decision that the conduct of both parties was "proper" under the circumstances does not necessarily decide the legal case; there could well be other reasons why one party should be preferred to another.

The point is illustrated by the famous case of *Vincent v. Lake Erie Transport. Co.* [16] During a violent storm, defendant ordered his men to continue to make the ship fast to the dock during the course of the storm in order to protect it from the elements. The wind and waves repeatedly drove it into the dock, damaging it to the extent of $500. Although there had been a prior contract between the plaintiff and the defendant, the case was treated by the court as though the parties to the suit were strangers, since the terms of the contract did not cover the incident in question. [17] Moreover, it was accepted without question that the conduct of the defendant was reasonable in that there was no possible course of action open to the captain of the ship that would have enabled him to reduce the aggregate damage suffered by the ship and the dock. On these facts the court concluded that the defendant had to pay the plaintiff for the $500 damage.

The result in *Vincent* seems inconsistent with either of the customary explanations, moral or economic, of negligence in the law of tort. There is no argument that the conduct of the defendant was "blameworthy" in any sense. The coercion on him was great, even though not imposed by some human agency. Any person in the position of the defendant's captain would have made

---

[16] 109 Minn. 456, 124 N.W. 221 (1910).

[17] Given that the parties had entered into contractual relations before the storm arose, it is possible to argue that the case should be disposed of on the ground that the plaintiff assumed the risk of damages in question. Indeed, the dissent appears to make that argument when it states that "one who constructs a dock to the navigable line of waters, and enters into contractual relations with the owner of a vessel to moor the same, takes the risk of damage to his dock by a boat caught there in a storm, which could not have been avoided by the exercise of due care." 109 Minn. at 461, 124 N.W. at 222. Of course, if the defense of assumption of risk were available on the facts, then there would be no reason to reach the difficult questions of private necessity and inevitable accident.

the same choice under the circumstances. It is true that he knew that his conduct could damage the dock, but nonetheless the necessity of the situation would serve as an adequate defense against any charge of intentional wrongdoing. Similarly, if the economic conception of negligence is adopted, the same result must be reached once it is admitted that the conduct of the defendant served to minimize the total amount of damage suffered; the expected benefits of further precautions were outweighed by their costs.

Had the Lake Erie Transportation Company owned both the dock and the ship, there could have been no lawsuit as a result of the incident. The Transportation Company, now the sole party involved, would, when faced with the storm, apply some form of cost-benefit analysis in order to decide whether to sacrifice its ship or its dock to the elements. Regardless of the choice made, it would bear the consequences and would have no recourse against anyone else. There is no reason why the company as a defendant in a lawsuit should be able to shift the loss in question because the dock belonged to someone else. The action in tort in effect enables the injured party to require the defendant to treat the loss he has inflicted on another as though it were his own. If the Transportation Company must bear all the costs in those cases in which it damages its own property, then it should bear those costs when it damages the property of another. The necessity may justify the decision to cause the damage, but it cannot justify a refusal to make compensation for the damage so caused.

The argument is not limited to the case where the defendant acts with the certain knowledge that his conduct will cause harm to others. It applies with equal force to cases where the defendant acts when he knows that there is only a *risk* that he will cause harm to others. In *Morris v. Platt,*[18] the plaintiff requested a jury instruction that the defendant should be found liable where he accidentally shot the plaintiff in an attempt to defend himself against an attack by third persons, even if he acted prudently under the circumstances. The court rejected that request and held instead that the plaintiff, even if an innocent bystander, could not recover for his injuries; the accident had been "inevitable."

Here I wish to concentrate upon only one difference between

[18]32 Conn. 75 (1864).

the two cases.[19] In *Morris* the only risk the defendant took was that his conduct would harm the plaintiff, while the defendant in *Vincent* knew that such harm would result as a matter of course. Regardless of the substantive theory of liability adopted, the cases cannot be distinguished on this ground.[20] Under the formula of *Carroll Towing,* the difference between the situations in *Morris* and in *Vincent* is taken into account in the "P" term in the formula. In *Vincent* the probability of harm (P) equals one, since the harm was certain. Hence the application of *Carroll Towing* to it turns only on the direct comparison between the burden of prevention (B) and the loss (L). In *Morris,* the application of that formula is somewhat more complex because "P" can take on any value between zero and one.

Morris, moreover, is not distinguishable from *Vincent* on any principled ground even if the *Carroll Towing* formula is rejected as the rule of substantive liability. In the discussion of *Vincent* the argument proceeded on the assumption that the defendant must bear the costs of those injuries that he inflicts upon others as though they were injuries that he suffered himself. The argument applies equally to cases where there is only the risk of harm. If the defendant in cases like *Morris* took the risk of injury to his own person or property, he would bear all the costs and enjoy all the benefits of that decision whether or not it was correct. That same result should apply where a person "only" takes risks with the person or property of other individuals.[21] There is no need to look

---

[19]See p. 32, *infra,* for a discussion of the relationship between the plea of compulsion by a third person and the plea of necessity.

[20]Seavey appears to take the opposite view in his discussion of the risk principle in negligence cases. Thus, he argues that some of the elements to be balanced in negligence cases "are not considered when the actor knows or desires that his conduct will result in interference with the plaintiff or his property. Thus if, to save his life, A intentionally destroys ten cents worth of B's property, A must pay; if, however, he takes a ten per cent chance of killing B in an effort to save his own life, his conduct might not be found wrongful, although obviously B would much prefer, antecedently, to lose ten cents worth of property than to submit to a ten per cent chance of being killed." Warren A. Seavey, Negligence—Subjective or Objective? 41 Harv. L. Rev. 1, 8, n. 7 (1927).

[21]"But so long as it is an element of imposed liability that the wrongdoer shall in some degree disregard the sufferer's interests, it can only be an anomaly, and indeed vindictive, to make him responsible to those whose interests he has not disregarded." Sinran v. Penn. R.R., 61 F.2d 767, 770 (2d Cir. 1932) (Judge Hand). The hard question is why one man should ever be permitted to "disregard the sufferer's interests."

at the antecedent risk once the harm has come to pass; no need to decide, without guide or reference, which risks are "undue" and which are not. If the defendant harms the plaintiff, then he should pay even if the risk he took was reasonable, just as he should pay in cases of certain harm where the decision to injure was reasonable.[22]

---

[22]Bohlen argues that the defense of necessity should be admitted when the defendant seeks to protect not only his own interests but those of society, on the ground that "one who acts as a champion of the public should be required to pay for the privilege of so doing." Francis H. Bohlen, Incomplete Privilege to Inflict Intentional Invasions of Interests of Property and Personality, 39 Harv. L. Rev. 307, 317–18 (1926). But there is no reason why the plaintiff should be required to bear that loss either. It is true, as Bohlen suggests, that the ideal solution may be to have the society as a whole bear those costs, but that prospect does not help in the resolution of the case as between these two parties to the suit.

III. An Analysis of Causation

Implicit in the development of the prior arguments is the assumption that the term "causation" has a content which permits its use in a principled manner to help solve particular cases. In order to make good on these arguments, that concept must be explicated and shown to be a suitable basis for the assignment of reponsibility. Those two ends can be achieved only if much of the standard rhetoric on causation in negligence cases is first put to one side.

Under the orthodox view of negligence, the question of causation is resolved by a two-step process. The first part of the inquiry concerns the "cause in fact" of the plaintiff's injury. The usual test to determine whether or not the plaintiff's injury was in fact caused by the negligence of the defendant is to ask whether, "but for the negligence of the defendant, the plaintiff would not have been injured." But this complex proposition is not in any sense the semantic equivalent of the assertion that the defendant caused the injury to the plaintiff. The former expression is in counterfactual form and requires an examination of what *would have* been the case if things had been otherwise.[1] The second expression simply asks in direct indicative form what in fact *did* happen. The change in mood suggests the difference between the two concepts.

The "but for" test does not provide a satisfactory account of the concept of causation if the words "in fact" are taken seriously. *A* carelessly sets his alarm one hour early. When he wakes up the next morning, he has ample time before work and decides to take an early morning drive in the country. While on the road he is

---

[1]The expression "things had been otherwise" is used because at this point in the analysis, it is not clear that the negligence in question refers to the doing of things that ought not to be done, or the failure to do those things that should be done, or both. The consequences that flow from the distinction are discussed at length in chap. IV.

spotted by *B*, an old college roommate, who becomes so excited that he runs off the road and hurts *C*. But for the negligence of *A*, *C* would never have been injured, because *B* doubtless would have continued along his uneventful way. Nonetheless, it is common ground that *A*, even if negligent, is in no way responsible for the injury to *C*, caused by *B*.

Its affinity for absurd hypotheticals should suggest that the "but for" test should be abandoned as even a tentative account of the concept of causation. But there has been no such abandonment. Instead it has been argued that the "but for" test provides a "philosophical" test for the concept of causation which shows that the "consequences" of any act (or at least any negligent act) extend indefinitely into the future.[2] But there is no merit, philosophic or otherwise, to an account of any concept which cannot handle the simplest of cases, and only a mistaken view of philosophic inquiry demands an acceptance of an account of causation that conflicts so utterly with ordinary usage.

Once the "philosophical" account of causation was accepted, it could not be applied in legal contexts without modification because of the unacceptable results that it required. The concept of "cause in law" or "proximate" cause[3] became necessary to confine the concept within acceptable limits.[4] In the earlier

---

[2] "Everybody is now in accord that *logically* there is no escape from the doctrine of the equivalence of conditions, according to which a defendant's conduct must be held to have caused damage if but for that conduct, however remotely connected with it, it would not have occurred: and that everything that ensues from it to the bitter end is its consequences." F. H. Lawson, Negligence in the Civil Law 53 (1950) (emphasis added). "In a philosophical sense, the consequences of an act go forward to eternity, and the causes of an event go back to the discovery of America and beyond." William L. Prosser, Handbook on the Law of Torts 236 (4th ed. 1971).

[3] The term proximate cause comes from one of Bacon's maxims. "In jure non remota causa sed proxima spectatur." (In law not the remote but only the proximate cause is looked to.) In many discussions, however, the term "legal" cause is used in the hope that it will be less misleading than "proximate cause." See Robert E. Keeton, Legal Cause in the Law of Tort, viii (1963). But the use of the term "legal" serves to establish a false opposition between its technical and its ordinary use, which again hampers the development of a theory that is both intuitively sensible and technically sound.

[4] In a separate but related development, the concept of "duty of care" was in the alternative invoked to limit the concept of "but for" causation. See Palsgraf v. Long Is. R.R. 248 N.Y. 339, 162 N.E. 99 (1928). "The nightmare of unlimited liability [on causal grounds] possessed most judges and most legal writers. To meet this doctrinal crisis the *duty* concept has been developed and where accepted has greatly cleared the jungle of negligence law." Leon Green, Foreseeability in

literature there was an attempt to work out in great detail specifications of the kinds of events and acts which would serve to break the causal connection between the conduct of the defendant and the harm suffered by the plaintiff.[5] That inquiry is indeed a necessary one in some cases, although it need not be tied to the concept of "but for" causation. In recent years, the inquiry has been continued and refined by Hart and Honoré in their classic work, *Causation in the Law*.[6] Hart and Honoré do not accept the "but for" account of causation, but instead define causation in a manner which recognizes the kinds of intervening acts and events that are to be taken into account before it can be shown that the conduct of the defendant was the cause of the plaintiff's harm; thus they argue that "an act is the cause of harm if it is an intervention in the course of affairs which is sufficient to produce the harm without the cooperation of the voluntary acts of others or abnormal conjunctions of events."[7] This definition and its careful explication, however, have been rejected for the most part in the legal literature on the ground that they require courts to confront "the never-ending and insoluble problems of causation,"[8] "together with the subtleties of *novus actus interveniens*."[9] In its stead, the question of proximate cause has been said to reduce itself to the question whether the conduct of the defendant is a "substantial factor"[10] contributing to the loss of the plaintiff, or whether the harm suffered was "reasonably foreseeable."[11] But

---

Negligence Law, 61 Colum. L. Rev. 1401, 1408 (1961). Although the reason for the introduction of the concept is clear, its place in the tort law is not, once "but for" is abandoned as an account of causation.

[5]See pp. 39–44, *infra*.

[6]H. L. A. Hart & A. M. Honoré, Causation in the Law (1959).

[7]*Id*. at 426.

[8]Overseas Tankship (U. K.) Ltd. v. Morts Dock & Engineering Co. Ltd. (The Wagon Mound), [1961] A. C. 388, 423 (N.S.W.).

[9]Glanville Williams, The Risk Principle, 77 L.Q. Rev. 179 (1961).

[10]Restatement of Torts 2d § 431, § 433, § 435 (1965); Clarence Morris, Studies in the Law of Torts 256–57 (1952).

[11]"Prima facie at least, the reasons for creating liability should limit it." Warren A. Seavey, Mr. Justice Cardozo and the Law of Torts, 52 Harv. L. Rev. 372, 386; 48 Yale L.J. 390, 404; 39 Colum. L. Rev. 20, 34 (1939). If negligence is accepted as a necessary precondition for liability in torts, then the argument has some appeal, because the defendant is regarded as negligent only if he has created a "reasonably foreseeable" risk of harm to another. Those who favored "directness" as the test

these formulations of the test of proximate cause do not give much guidance for the solution of particular cases.[12] One might think that this would be treated as a defect in an account of a concept like causation, but in large measure it has been thought to be its strength. Once it is decided that there is no hard content to the term causation, the courts are free to decide particular lawsuits in accordance with the principles of "social policy" under the guise of the proximate-cause doctrine.

But it is false to argue that systems of law that use the principles of causation to decide cases must stand in opposition to those systems that use principles of social policy to achieve that same end. As Hart and Honoré have pointed out, the major premise of most legal systems (until perhaps the recent past) is that causation provides, *as a matter of policy,* the reason to decide cases in one way rather than the other.[13] Moreover, they properly observe:

> It is fatally easy and has become increasingly common to make the transition from the exhilarating discovery that complex words like "cause" cannot be simply defined and have no "one true meaning"

---

for remoteness of damages within a negligence framework have always had to concede that reasonable foresight was the test for liability.

The presence or absence of reasonable anticipation of damage determines the legal quality of the act as negligent or innocent. If it be thus determined to be negligent, then the question whether particular damages are recoverable depends only on the answer to the question whether they are the direct consequence of the act.

In re Polemis, [1921] 3 K.B. 560, 574 (C.A.). But once negligence is rejected as the basis for civil liability in tort, the argument of symmetry works in the opposite direction. If foresight (and negligence) are no longer treated as material on the question of liability, then they should be immaterial on the question of remoteness of damage. There is no need to worry about endless liability because "but for" is never used as the test of causation, as it is in the conventional negligence analysis. Robert E. Keeton, *supra* note 3, at viii (1963).

[12]Under the foresight test the distinction between the "general kind" of damages and "its precise details," becomes crucial. See Glanville Williams, *supra* note 9, at 183–85. But the application of that distinction presupposes that we have already selected the *description* of the events in question to which that distinction is applied. But without a standard means to select the unique description, it cannot be determined whether the unforeseeable aspects of the case fall on one side of the line or the other. This is the dilemma: Foresight is not psychologically irrelevant to the solution of problems of remoteness and often affects the judgment of those who try them. Yet foresight cannot function as a test until the facts of the case are described, and since the facts are nearly always susceptible of differing descriptions which will vary the result, a foresight criterion cannot function in a true testing process. Clarence Morris, *supra* note 10, at 260.

[13]H. L. A. Hart & A. M. Honoré, *supra* note 6, at 58–64.

> to the mistaken conclusion that they have no meaning worth bothering about at all, but are used as a mere disguise for arbitrary decision or judicial policy. This is blinding error, and legal language and reasoning will never develop while it persists.[14]

But for all their force these remarks have not received general acceptance. Indeed, once it was agreed that the term "proximate cause" gave the courts room to engage in creative decisions of social policy, the next step was not hard to take. If the term "proximate cause" only masks the underlying policy considerations, then academic literature, which need not even pay lip service to precedent, should cast it aside to deal with the policy considerations in their own terms. Thus, in *The Costs of Accidents,* Guido Calabresi uses the tools of economic analysis to develop a comprehensive theory that will provide an adequate framework to test and develop the substantive rules of tort liability. The author makes clear that he does not think the concept of causation plays any part in the development of his theory. He describes "cause" as a "weasel word" and claims that he "does not propose to consider the question of what, if anything, we mean when we say that specific activities 'cause,' in some metaphysical sense, a given accident; in fact, when we identify an act or activity as a 'cause,' we may be expressing any number of ideas."[15] But the term cannot be banished from the lexicon on the ground that it is "metaphysical." The concept is dominant in the law because it is dominant in the language that people, including lawyers, use to describe conduct and to determine responsibility.[16] The importance of the concept is revealed when Calabresi discusses at length the question of "what-is-a-cost-of-what" in two chapters that address themselves to the question of "which activities cause which accident costs." The concept may not be strictly necessary to the development of some theory of tort if the goal of the system is the minimization of the costs of accidents. But its presence reminds us that a system of law which tries to banish it from use may not respond to ordinary views on individual blame and accountability.

This last point is brought home by an examination of another skeptical account of causation. In *The Problem of Social Cost,*

---

[14]*Id.* at 3.

[15]Guido Calabresi, The Costs of Accidents 6–7, n. 8 (1970).

[16]H. L. A. Hart & A. M. Honoré, *supra* note 6, at 59–62.

Professor Coase argues that the concept of causation, as he understands it, does not permit the solution of individual legal disputes.[17] Although he does not work from the "but for" paradigm, he does adopt a model of causation that treats as a cause of a given harm any *joint condition* necessary to its creation. Since the acts of both parties are "necessary," it follows that the concept of causation provides, in this analysis, no grounds to prefer either person to another. The problem is "reciprocal" in both causal and economic terms. In effect, Coase argues that the harms in question resulted because two persons each wished to make inconsistent uses of a common resource:

> The question is commonly thought of as one in which A inflicts harm on B and what has to be decided is: how should we restrain A? But this is wrong. We are dealing with a problem of a reciprocal nature. To avoid the harm to B would inflict harm on A. The real question that has to be decided is: should A be allowed to harm B or should B be allowed to harm A? The problem is to avoid the more serious harm. I instanced in my previous article the case of a confectioner the noise and vibrations from whose machinery disturbed a doctor in his work. To avoid harming the doctor would inflict harm on the confectioner. The problem posed by this case was essentially whether it was worth while, as a result of restricting the methods of production which could be used by the confectioner, to secure more doctoring at the cost of a reduced supply of confectionery products. Another example is afforded by the problem of straying cattle which destroy crops on neighbouring land. If it is inevitable that some cattle will stray, an increase in the supply of meat can only be obtained at the expense of a decrease in the supply of crops. The nature of the choice is clear: meat or crops. What answer should be given is, of course, not clear unless we know the value of what is obtained as well as the value of what is sacrificed to obtain it. To give another example, Professor George J. Stigler instances the contamination of a stream. If we assume that the harmful effect of the pollution is that it kills the fish, the question to be decided is: is the value of the fish lost greater or less than the value of the product which the contamination of the stream makes possible.[18]

In the first portion of this paragraph, Professor Coase argues that the question is reciprocal because "to avoid the harm to *A* would

---

[17]Ronald H. Coase, The Problem of Social Cost, 3 J. Law & Econ. 1 (1960). The criticisms made of Coase's position in the text are limited to his account of the concept of causation. I accept his economic analysis.
[18]*Id.* at 2.

be to inflict harm upon *B*." The real question is "should *A* be allowed to harm *B* or should *B* be allowed to harm *A*." But that image of reciprocity is not carried through in the concrete description of particular cases used to support the general proposition. The first case concerns a "confectioner the noise and vibrations from whose machinery *disturbed* a doctor"; the second, "straying cattle . . . *destroy* crops on neighboring land"; in the third, "the harmful effect of the pollution . . . *kills* the fish." Coase describes each situation by the use of sentences that differentiate between the role of the *subject* of each of these propositions and the role of the *object*. There is no question but that the confectioner harmed the doctor; the cattle the crops; and the contaminants, the fish. The problem only takes on a *guise* of reciprocity when the party harmed seeks his remedy in court. To use but the first example, the doctor wishes to call in aid the court to "harm" the confectioner, in the sense that he wishes to restrain him from acting to harm his practice. But he is justified in so doing because of the harm the confectioner either has inflicted or will inflict upon him. It would be a grave mistake to say that *before* the invocation of judicial remedies the grounds of dispute disclosed reciprocal harm. The confectioner did not seek to enjoin the doctor from the practice of medicine, because that practice did not and could not harm the confectioner. The notion of causal reciprocity should not be confused with the notion of redress for harm caused.[19]

Both Calabresi and Coase, then, share the belief that the concept of causation should not, because it cannot, play any role in the determination of liability for harms that have occurred. The pages that follow are designed to show that the concept of causation, as it applies to cases of physical injury, can be analyzed in a matter that both renders it internally coherent and relevant to the ultimate question who shall bear the loss.

There will be no attempt to give a single semantic equivalent to the

[19]The importance of reciprocity to questions of responsibility is developed in George P. Fletcher, Fairness and Utility in Tort Theory, 85 Harv. L. Rev. 537 (1972). Fletcher argues that the principles of corrective justice require the law to impose liability for harm only where the defendant has exposed the plaintiff to a "nonreciprocal risk of injury," at least where the defendant is not otherwise excused. But Fletcher does not tell us how to determine whether two risks are reciprocal. Moreover, even if that determination could be made, its relevance is questionable once the harm has come to pass. Even if two risks were reciprocal, it does not follow that neither party should have his action when injured.

concept of causation. Instead, the paper will consider in succession each of four distinct paradigm cases covered by the proposition *"A* caused *B* harm." These paradigms are not the only way in which we can talk about torts cases. They do, however, provide modes of description which best capture the ordinary use of causal language. Briefly put, they are based upon notions of force, fright, compulsion and dangerous conditions. The first of them will be the simplest to analyze. Each of the subsequent paradigms will introduce further problems to be resolved before the judgment on the causal issue can be made. Nonetheless, despite the internal differences, it can, I believe, be demonstrated that each of these paradigms, when understood, exhibits the features that render it relevant to the question of legal responsibility.

Force. We begin with the simplest instance of causation: the application of force to a person or thing. In a physical sense, the consequences of the application of force may be quite varied. In some cases the object acted upon will move; in others it will be transformed; in still others it will be damaged. It is this last case that will be of exclusive concern here, because it is accepted without question that the minimum condition of tort liability is damage to the person or property of the plaintiff.

The identification of causation with force does not of itself complete the first instance of the proposition *"A* caused harm to *B."* It is still necessary to show that the force in question was applied by human and not natural agencies, and thus to tie the concept of force to that of human volition. The term "volition" is a primitive in the language whose function is to mark off the class of human acts from the class of events; to distinguish between "I raised my arm," and "my arm went up." But even if the term cannot be defined, its function can be made clear by some simple examples. In the old case of *Smith v. Stone,*[20] the defendant was carried on to the plaintiff's land by a band of armed men. The court held that the plaintiff could not recover in trespass, because it was "the trespasse of the party that carried the defendant upon the land, and not the trespasse of the defendant." True, the physical requirement of entrance was satisfied in the case, but the defendant's movement was in no sense an "action" because, if anything, it was contrary to his will.

[20]Style 65, 82 Eng. Rep. 533 (1647).

Only if some concept of volition is accepted into the language will there be a means to distinguish this case from one in which the defendant *entered* upon the land. In another early case, it was noted that "if a man by force take my hand and strike you," I could not be held liable in trespass because my hand was only the instrument of some other person who, in fact, caused the harm.[21] These two examples should be sufficient to show that we cannot do without the term "volition," even if it cannot be defined. But one need not apologize for its use, because there is no alternative system for the description of human conduct or the assignment of responsibility that can do without the term, including those which turn on negligence, either in its moral or economic interpretation, when they ask what the defendant "could have" done. The concept of "volition" is thus crucial in those theories as well, even if it (along with the notion of force) can never be dispositive on questions of legal responsibility.[22]

The combination of force and volition is expressed in the simple transitive sentence, *A hit B*. It is true that this proposition as stated is consistent with the assertion that *A* did not harm *B*. But in many contexts the implication of harm follows fairly from the assertion, as anyone hit by a car will admit. Where the issue is in doubt, the verb can be changed, even as the form of the proposition remains constant, to bring the element of harm more sharply into relief. Thus instead of *"A hit B,"* another proposition of the requisite form could be *"A pummeled B,"* or *"A beat B."* But since the specifics of the harm go only to the measure of damages and not to the issue of liability, the proposition *"A hit B"* will serve as the model of the class of propositions to be considered.

The grammatical structure of the proposition *"A hit B"* is crucial to analysis of the problem of causation because it describes a situation both where the parties are *linked* to each other and where their respective roles are still *differentiated*. When causation is defined in this manner, the roles of the parties, contrary to Coase, are not reciprocal. The proposition that *"A hit B"* cannot be treated as synonymous with the proposition that *"B hit A."*

---

[21]Weaver v. Ward, Hobart 134, 80 Eng. Rep. 284 (1616).

[22]See, *e.g.,* Fowler v. Lanning, [1959] 1 Q.B. 426, dismissing an action where "the statement of claim alleges laconically that . . . the defendant shot the plaintiff." *Id.* at 431.

Each of these propositions is complete without reference to either further acts, whether or not voluntary, or to natural events, whether or not abnormal. Questions of intervention are not present, and hence there are no problems about the coordination of multiple actions or events to determine responsibility for a single harm. But it may well be necessary as a matter of fact to assess the role of those forces that are the *instruments* of the defendant. Take a simple case where *A* drives his car into *B*. It could be argued that *A*'s act extended no further than the depression of the gas pedal or, perhaps, *A*'s movement of his leg muscles.[23] But the constant and inveterate use of the English language militates against the restriction of an act to the physical movements of *A*'s body. "*A* drove his car into *B*" is a true description of the event; we might explain its significance away, but we can never deny it in good faith. Reference to those subsequent mechanical complications does not falsify that description. The use of the simple transitive proposition confirms the judgment that these subsequent mechanical occurrences are but the *means*, and nothing more, which *A* used to move his car.[24]

Finally, the proposition of the form "*A* hit *B*" does not depend upon the two-part theory of causation developed by the law of negligence. No question of "but for" is ever raised, much less answered. It may well be that "but for the blow of the plaintiff

---

[23]Holmes took the extreme position: "An act is always a voluntary muscular contraction, and nothing else. The chain of physical sequences which it sets in motion or directs to the plaintiff's harm is no part of it, and very generally a long train of such sequences intervenes. . . . When a man commits an assault and battery with a pistol, his only act is to contract the muscles of his arm and forefinger in a certain way, but it is the delight of elementary writers to point out what a vast series of physical changes must take place before the harm is done." O. W. Holmes, *supra* chap. II, note 4, at 91.

Holmes developed this position in order to show that the distinction between trespass and case no longer had substantive importance once the forms of action were abolished. That distinction will, however, be defended, but not on the traditional grounds that liability in trespass was strict, while that in case is predicated on negligence or on intent to harm. P. 47, *infra*.

[24]The case would be different if *A* parked his car where it was pushed by *C*'s car into *B*. *C* did not act as the instrument of *A* and the question of the assignment of responsibility among several actors must be fairly confronted. The difference between the two cases is reflected in the language, because there is no simple transitive verb structure in English of the form "*A* hit *B*" that describes the case just put. It will not do at this point to say that "*A* caused harm to *B*," because thus far the term causation only covers propositions like *A* hit *B*. See pp. 32–35, *infra*.

the harm never would have occurred"; but it is not the "but for" test which establishes the causal preeminence of the application of force by the defendant to the person or property of the plaintiff. Since, moreover, the "but for" test was not used to establish cause in fact, there is no further issue to be discussed under the guise of proximate cause; the false opposition between cause in fact and proximate cause thus disappears.

Once this simple causal paradigm is accepted, its relationship to the question of responsibility for the harm so caused must be clarified. Briefly put, the argument is that proof of the proposition A hit B should be sufficient to establish a prima facie case of liability.[25] I do not argue that proof of causation is equivalent to a conclusive demonstration of responsibility.[26] Both the modern and classical systems of law are based upon the development of prima facie cases and defenses thereto. They differ not in their use of presumptions but in the elements needed to create the initial presumption in favor of the plaintiff. The doctrine of strict liability holds that proof that the defendant caused harm creates that presumption because proof of the nonreciprocal source of the harm is sufficient to upset the balance where one person must win and the other must lose. There is no room to consider, as part of the prima facie case, allegations that the defendant intended to harm the plaintiff, or could have avoided the harm he caused by the use of reasonable care. The choice is plaintiff or defendant, and the analysis of causation is the tool which, prima facie, fastens responsibility upon the defendant. Indeed for most persons, the difficult question is often not whether these causal assertions create the presumption, but whether there are in fact any means to distinguish between causation and responsibility, so close is the connection between what a man does and what he is answerable for.

These arguments, however abstract in form, do have concrete application. Many cases will be decided in the same way regard-

[25]The argument depends upon "a deep sense of common law morality that one who hurts another should compensate him." Leon Green, *supra* note 4, at 1412.

[26]This should serve to answer those who argue that a system of strict liability is an "unmoral" system of tort. James Barr Ames, *supra* chap. II, note 3, at 97. The truth of such an assertion depends upon an assessment of the complete system including all excuses and justifications. For example, one would have a different view of the rules of strict liability if self-defense were never admitted as a justification for the harm caused. *Ibid.*

less of the theory adopted, but the choice of theory in some instances can determine both the outcome of the case and the kinds of proof relevant to its decision. Such a case is *Bolton v. Stone*.[27] There a batsman in a cricket match hit an unusually long ball which carried clear of the fence that surrounded the defendant's cricket grounds and struck the plaintiff in the head while she stood on the adjoining highway. She brought an action against the owners of the grounds for her personal injuries. But she was confronted by the rule that allows recovery only if the plaintiff can plead and prove that the defendant acted with either negligence or an intent to harm.[28] Neither the cricket club nor the batsman meant the plaintiff any harm. To the extent that liability rested upon the single act of the batsman, it was clear that no allegation of negligence could be sustained, for before the blow the risk his activity created to the plaintiff was very small. This left the question whether the cricket club had maintained its grounds in a reasonable and safe condition, given the use to which they were dedicated. The plaintiff tried to show that it was incumbent upon the club to take some precautions to ensure that no cricket balls escaped from the grounds. But the House of Lords in its application of the rules of "reasonable foresight" decided that the defendant had breached no duty of care to the plaintiff. At points the position of the House of Lords appears reminiscent of Learned Hand's opinion in *Carroll Towing*. Thus Lord Reid stated, "In my judgment the test to be applied here is whether the risk of damage to a person on the road was so small that a reasonable man in the position of the appellants, considering the matter from the point of view of safety, would have thought it right to refrain from taking steps to prevent the danger."[29]

But even if the decision is consistent with the "reasonable foresight" test, it was not reached with either assurance or comfort by the House of Lords. The trial court had decided the case for the defendants, but had been reversed by a split vote in the court of

[27][1951] A.C. 850.

[28]"Whatever may have been the law of England in early times, I am of the opinion that as the law now stands an allegation of negligence is in general essential to the relevancy of an action of reparation for personal injuries." Read v. Lyons & Co. Ltd., [1947] A.C. 156, 170–71 (Lord MacMillan).

[29][1951] A.C. 850, at 867.

appeal, before the House of Lords restored the original verdict. Lord Oaksey called it a "difficult" case;[30] Lord Reid gave it "repeated and anxious consideration";[31] Lord Normand noted that the whole issue was "fairly balanced."[32] Lord Radcliffe stated in the course of his opinion in the case that "he could see nothing unfair in the appellants being required to compensate the respondent for the serious injury that she received as a result of the sport that they have organized, but the law of negligence is concerned less with what is fair than with what is culpable. . . ."[33]

Nor was the concern with result confined to the judges who decided the case. For example, Professor Goodhart, one of the staunchest supporters of the negligence requirement, entitled his comment on *Bolton v. Stone* "Is it cricket?" and wondered if the case were wrongly decided, since defendant could have altered the location of the cricket field.[34] Again, in response to public concern, the Cricket Clubs of England, which had supported the appeal to the House of Lords, announced that they had taken all steps necessary to ensure that Miss Stone did not suffer the financial consequences of her injury.[35]

In light of its aftermath, it has been suggested that *Bolton v. Stone* is one of a small class of cases where it is both "right and proper" for the defendant to make compensation even though under no legal obligation to do so.[36] The irony of this position

[30]*Id.* at 863.

[31]*Id.* at 867.

[32]*Id.* at 861.

[33]*Id.* at 868. See Abraham Harari, *supra* chap. II, note 14, at 175-76, for a detailed analysis of the difficulties of Lord Radcliffe's statement.

[34]67 L.Q. Rev. 460, 463 (1951). Professor Goodhart dismissed the possibility that the defendant was under a duty to increase the height of the fence around the grounds. "The fact that the absence of such a fence might be negligence in the case of a low bouncing ball, does not make it negligence in the case of a direct high hit." *Id.* at 463. This last observation illustrates anew the difficulty of identifying "the" risk in negligence cases against which there is a duty to guard.

[35]The *Economist* and the daily newspapers made something of a cause célèbre out of the case, because Miss Stone, under the English system of costs, was obligated to pay more than £3000 in court costs after she lost in the House of Lords. 67 L.Q. Rev. 461. The Cricket Clubs that supported the appeal assured the readers of Law Quarterly Review that the Cricket Club permitted Miss Stone to retain the costs and damages paid to her after the decision in her favor in the Court of Appeal. Notes, 68 L.Q. Rev. 3-4 (1952).

[36]"[O]ne who is under no legal liability for damage caused to another may yet

should be apparent. *Bolton v. Stone* is an easy case under the rules of strict liability. The plaintiff's conduct provides no defense for the defendant, once the prima facie case, *A* hit *B*, is proved. There is no cleavage between the legal result and the ethical sentiment. Only where a theory of negligence is adopted is it necessary to "explain" this case in terms of some notion of "ethical" compensation. Only "unmoral" theory of strict liability in the end produces the proper result.

Moreover, the shift in thinking from trespass to negligence serves to change the entire complexion of the arguments in the case. Under a pure trespass theory, the defendant is the batsman who hit the ball that struck the plaintiff.[37] The paradigm of "*A* hit *B*" applies without question to the case. But since trespassory notions were rejected in *Bolton v. Stone*, the plaintiff had to make a case against the defendant on the theory that its cricket grounds were negligently maintained[38] and this opened up a vast range of questions—on the appropriate size for the cricket field; the location of the pitch; the height of the fence; the year the cricket club began to use its grounds; the land use patterns in the neighborhood both at and since that time;[39] the number of cricket balls hit

---

think it right and proper to offer some measure of compensation." John Salmond, *supra* chap. II, note 2, at 30 (13th ed., 1961). The supporting footnote cites *Bolton v. Stone* as an instance of such a case. This notion of "ethical compensation" was first advanced by Glanville Williams, The Aims of the Law of Tort, 4 Curr. Legal Probs. 137, 142 (1951). But Williams does not favor the rules of strict liability, which would eliminate the need for the notion of "ethical compensation." See note 9 *supra*.

[37]Lord Porter noted that the defendants, who were the trustees of the field, admitted that they were "responsible for the negligent actions of those who use the field in the way intended that it be used." [1951] A.C. at 858. But once the action is brought on a trespass theory, the principle of vicarious liability must be invoked before either cricket club could be sued. That principle applies easily enough to the team which employed the batsman. In *Bolton v. Stone*, however, the defendants were the trustees of the home team while the batsman was a member of the visiting team. Hence, in a sense, the result in the case might be correct after all.

[38]The question of liability in trespass was raised in John Salmond, *supra* chap. II, note 2, at 194, n.76 (13th ed., 1961). A claim based upon a nuisance theory was not pursued to the House of Lords. [1951] A.C. at 868.

[39]Beckenham Road, where the plaintiff was standing when hit, had been built in 1910, while the Cricket Club had used its field since 1864. [1951] A.C. at 851. The House of Lords rejected the argument that some precautions should have been taken, or the matter at least considered, when the road was made. *Id.* at 862 (Lord Normand). But it is not clear how this particular piece of information is relevant under the *Carroll Towing* formula.

into Mr. Brownson's neighboring garden;[40] the number hit into the street; the defendants' views about the safety of their own grounds. It cannot be a point in favor of the law of negligence, either as a theoretical or administrative matter, that it demands evaluation of almost everything, but can give precise weight to almost nothing.

Fright and Shock. The structure of the prima facie case for assault—the historical companion to trespass to the person[41] —parallels the paradigm for the prima facie case of the tort of trespass, and illustrates the means by which the concept of causation can be extended in a principled manner. The case in assault is *A* frightened *B*. That paradigm indicates, as in trespass, that *A* and *B* do not have symmetrical roles. There is the same close connection between the conduct of the defendant and the harm of the plaintiff. There is, however, a difference between the cases of assault and those of trespass. In trespass actions the plaintiff's conduct is not in issue in the prima facie case. But the *reactions* of the plaintiff must be taken into account before the prima facie case of assault can be completed. Still, the roles of the parties are not identical. The reactions of the plaintiff do not rise to the level of acts because they are in no sense volitional.

Nonetheless, the paradigm does raise some troublesome issues. Suppose, for example, the defendant frightened the plaintiff when he raised his hand to mop the sweat off his face at a time when the plaintiff was standing about fifty yards away. Do facts such as these disclose a prima facie case of assault? Our first response to the allegation does not address the issue of substantive

---

[40]Nor do I think that the respondent improves her case by proving that a number of balls were hit into Mr. Brownson's garden. It is danger to persons in the road, not to Mr. Brownson or his visitors, which is being considered. [1951] A.C. at 859 (Lord Porter). It is not quite clear whether it was material that the garden was closer to the field than the place where Miss Stone stood. *Id.* at 861. See also Glanville Williams, *supra* note 9, at 188.

[41]The relationship is not always regarded as significant today. Thus, in one of the recent casebooks on the law of tort, the specific discussion of the tort of assault has been removed from its traditional place beside the tort of battery to a point in the text where it is considered in conjunction with the more modern torts concerned with defamation and the right of privacy. Charles O. Gregory & Harry Kalven, Jr., Cases and Materials on Torts (2d ed. 1969). Although there may well be pedagogical justifications for the shift of materials within a casebook, there are strong reasons as a matter of theory why assaults should be examined in conjunction with trespasses.

29

law at all. Rather, it says that the harm suffered by the plaintiff is so trivial that it is inappropriate to use, at public expense, the legal machinery to resolve the case. Such a rule, of course, applies with full force both to theories of strict liability and to those of negligence and intent, and does not help choose between theories when both are applicable.

But the case can be made more difficult by assuming that the plaintiff has suffered serious injuries as a result of his fright. If anyone could be frightened by that kind of conduct, however, most likely he could not have survived long enough in life's hustle and bustle to be injured by the defendant. Thus in a sense, the initial statement of fact turns out to be simply unbelievable even where it is assumed for the sake of argument. In cases like these the defendant should be able to deny the allegation contained in the prima facie case, and be able to claim with some truth that the plaintiff had induced his own fright.[42]

But even after these odd cases are put to one side, the paradigm of assault does raise problems of proof that are not present in trespass cases since the allegation "*A* frightened *B*," unlike the allegation "*A* hit *B*," can be proved in the given case only after the responses of *B* are taken into account. *Courvoisier v. Raymond*[43] puts the issue well, even though it is the *defendant* who raises the issue of assault as an affirmative defense. The plaintiff was a plainclothesman who was sent to investigate at the scene of a riot in a small frontier town; the defendant was the owner of a store which had already been robbed several times during the course of the evening. When the defendant saw the plaintiff, he thought that he intended to rob the store and shot him. Under a theory of strict liability, the statement of the prima facie case is

---

[42]The position in the text is not an altogether happy one even if sound. In order to escape the problem, it is possible to argue that the plaintiff should not be allowed to recover, even if frightened, because he was extrasensitive. This position, however, itself has difficulties because it is inconsistent with the position, which I defend in chap. IV, that the defendant must take his victim as he finds him. Nonetheless it is possible to recognize the defense in assault cases only, on the ground that in these cases the causal relationships can never be established with the clarity appropriate to physical injury cases. Thus it is the difficulties with the causal question that invite the recognition of the defense. Consistent with that position, it should be possible to limit the use of this defense to cases where there is no "substantial" ground for fright at all, because only there is the causal question difficult.

[43]23 Colo. 113, 47 Pac. 284 (1896).

evident: The defendant shot the plaintiff. The only difficult question concerns the existence of a defense which takes the form, the plaintiff assaulted the defendant. That question is a question of fact, and the jury found in effect that the plaintiff did not frighten the defendant into shooting him. Rather, the defendant either made the judgment to shoot the plaintiff in light of all that he knew about the situation or was frightened by the activities of third persons. One could, perhaps, quarrel with that determination, but at least the answer put is to the right question, a question that does not arise where physical invasions are in issue.

The result in *Courvoisier* was much less satisfactory when the case was taken on appeal. The court reverted to the traditional models that predicate responsibility on negligence or intent, and the choice of theories again affected the outcome of the case. The court held that the defendant should be given an opportunity to prove in justification of his act that he acted reasonably and in apparent self-defense given the riot, even though he intended to hurt the plaintiff. Unlike the court in *Vincent,* it allowed the defendant to shift his problems to the plaintiff.

The arguments for strict liability carry over from cases of trespass to cases of assault. Negligence and intent should be immaterial to the prima facie case of assault, and for the same reasons as with trespass. Nonetheless, the law in fright cases has followed the pattern of the physical injury cases and at a minimum has insisted that the defendant show either negligence or intent. Indeed, in many cases even the basic rules of negligence are hedged about with further limitations. Although the cases exhibit no consistent pattern, it has been held that the plaintiff is allowed to recover for his harm only if there was a physical trespass to the plaintiff,[44] or, in the alternative, a threat of physical injury.[45] In other cases, there is the strong suggestion that a person can recover in fright cases where he is not subject to threat of physical

---

[44]Victoria Rys. Commiss'rs v. Coultus, 13 App. Cas. 222 (P.C. 1888) (Vict.). The decision was rejected in England in Dulieu v. White, [1901] 2 K.B. 669.

[45]Waube v. Warrington, 216 Wis. 603, 258 N.W. 497 (1935). Bourhill v. Young, [1943] A.C. 92 (Scot.). *Waube* expressly relied on the duty limitation in the *Palsgraf* case, while the opinion of Lord Wright in *Bourhill* is reminiscent of *Palsgraf,* which however, is not cited. Both of those cases show how the "duty" requirement can operate to deny liability in cases where the question of causation, far from being philosophical, is simple.

injury only if he can show that some member of his immediate family was in danger of physical harm.[46]

It is true that all of these elements could well be material as a matter of evidence in a fright case. It may well be that a person is more apt to be shocked if he is in danger of physical injury, or if a member of his immediate family is in such danger. But they are only matters of evidence. The crucial question is that of causation, and if a defendant frightens or shocks a plaintiff, the recovery should, prima facie, be allowed even if none of the further conditions sometimes placed on recovery are satisfied.[47]

Compulsion. The concept of causation is not limited to cases of the form "*A* hit *B*" or "*A* frightened *B*." There are other relationships that exhibit more complex grammatical forms to which it also applies. Indeed, the proposition "*A* hit *B*" represents only a special case of a more complex relationship, capable of indefinite extension, which for three persons takes the form "*A* compelled *B* to hit *C*."[48]

Cases of this form are more difficult to treat than simple trespass cases, because the verb "compel" is not a simple transitive verb. It is rather an instance of a small class of verbs which are "hypertransitive" or "causative" in nature. The logical object of "compel" is not a person (or thing) as it is in the case of the proposition *A* hit *B* (or *B*'s car), but an embedded (and transformed)

---

[46]Thus, the remarks of Denning, L. J., as he then was, in King v. Phillips, [1953] 1 Q.B. 429, 441: "Some cases seem plain enough. A wife or mother who suffers shock on being told of an accident to a loved one cannot recover damages from the negligent party on that account. Nor can a bystander who suffers shock by witnessing an accident from a safe distance. . . . But if the bystander is a mother who suffers from shock by hearing or seeing, with her own unaided senses, that her child is in peril, then she may be able to recover from the negligent party, even though she was in no personal danger herself: Hambrook v. Stokes Brothers [(1925) 1 K.B. 141]." Lord Wright said that he agreed with that decision. So do I.

[47]These limitations could well be necessary but not as a matter of substantive theory, in order to control a flood of fraudulent and frivolous claims in the court. But if that is the problem, the techniques of procedure, evidence and jury control seem better suited to ensure exclusion of groundless claims.

[48]The most famous decided case of this form is Scott v. Shepherd, 2 Wm. Black. 892, 96 Eng. Rep. 525; 3 Wilson 403, 95 Eng. Rep. 1124 (1773). There four persons were involved in the chain of causation. Shepherd (the defendant) compelled Ryals to compel Willis to strike Scott. In principle the argument could be extended indefinitely, but there quickly comes a point where the truth, not the coherence, of the proposition comes into doubt.

proposition—*B* to hit *C*—which itself sets out a causal relationship between two persons.

In the discussion of the proposition "*A* hit *B*," it was noted that *A* and *B* assumed different positions in the proposition because of the different roles which they played. In the analysis of this more complex proposition and its relationship to the question of responsibility, there is the same interaction between non-reciprocity and causation as in the simple cases already analyzed. In order to unpack these relationships, consider the case from the standpoint of the injured party, *C*. If the proposition "*A* compelled *B* to hit *C*" is true, then it follows that "*B* hit *C*." The last proposition can be analyzed in accordance with the notions of causation based upon force and volition that have already been developed. Given that paradigm, it follows that *C* has a prima facie case against *B*. *B* cannot escape liability by showing that he did not hit *C*, for a demonstration that he acted under compulsion is not the same as a demonstration that he did not act at all: *Smith v. Stone* is a different case from *Vincent v. Lake Erie*. Nor, if the observations about the defense of "necessity" made earlier are sound, can *B* plead as a defense that he was compelled by *A* to hit *C*. Even if this conduct were reasonable, it does not follow that *B* need not pay. Nor is this result unfair: *Vincent v. Lake Erie* holds a person in *B*'s position liable for the harm he inflicts in cases of necessity even though the defendant has neither a defense nor an action over. *B* will have an action over against *A* after he has paid *C*, on the theory that *A* compelled him (to his loss) to hit *C*.[49]

The analysis is not yet complete, because *C* is not limited to an action against *B*. He can bring in the alternative an action against *A*. That action, however, could not rely on trespassory theories of causation. *A* did not hit *C*; *B* did. But the roles of *A* and *C* are still both linked, and differentiated, because *A* compelled *B* to hit *C*; *C* did not compel *B* to hit *A*. Coase's requirement of nonreciprocal conduct can be met here as well as in trespass cases, even after the intermediate act of *B* is taken into account. That act,

---

[49]Indeed, under the modern law, there is never a difficult question of causation at all in the action of *C* against *A*, perhaps in part because the "but for" analysis tends to overstate the linkage between events. Only with the kind of causation analysis developed here must the remoteness issue be confronted. If it must be shown that *B* acted with either negligence or intent, then *C* will have no action against *B*.

done under the compulsion of A, does not sever the causal connection, even if it changes the specific theory of relief in question. B in effect drops out of the picture in the action between A and C once it is shown that he has acted under compulsion.[50]

The changes in causal theory have their effect on questions of proof. Proof of compulsion upon B is crucial if C's action against A is to succeed. The inquiry on that issue, moreover, is more complex than those required under either of the two paradigms of causation already considered. In trespass cases, no conduct of the plaintiff had to be taken into account to complete the prima facie case. In assault cases, only the reactions of the plaintiff to the act of the defendant were material. Thus neither of these paradigm cases required the examination of an intermediate act.

In particular, two points must be observed. First, the question whether B was negligent under the circumstances is, at best, evidence on the question of compulsion. It may well be that a reasonable man would have acted differently under all the circumstances, including his peril. But this actor B may not be that man, and it is his conduct, not that of some legal construct, that is the subject of inquiry: where B was compelled by A, the prima facie case is made out, even if B was negligent. Second, it is not strictly material whether B intended to harm C, because he could have been compelled to act as he did whether or not that harm was intended. Nonetheless, where harm was intended by B, it must be determined that B did not use the act of A as a cloak or excuse to further his own private interests.

One further problem remains. Suppose C is able to bring actions against both A and B. He will not be entitled to a double recovery for the single harm, so it will be necessary to decide whether A or B will be saddled with the ultimate loss. Here again the causal paradigm permits us to link and differentiate the roles of the parties

---

[50]That result is often reached in an intuitive sense when acts performed under compulsion are said, inexactly, to be "involuntary," and hence "no acts at all." Raphael Powell, 'Novus Actus Interveniens' in Roman Law, 4 Curr. Legal Probs. 195 (1951). The affinity between cases under this last paradigm and those of trespass is illustrated by the resort to simple transitive verbs in the declaration in *Scott v. Shepherd:* "Trespass and assault for throwing, casting, and tossing a lighted squib at and against the plaintiff, and *striking* him therewith on the face and so *burning* one of his eyes, that he lost the sight of it, whereby. . . ." 2 Wm. Black. 892, 96 Eng. Rep. 525 (1773) (emphasis added).

to the suit. *A* compelled *B* to hit *C*; *B* did not compel *A* to hit *C*. Hence it follows that, prima facie, *B* should prevail over *A*.

When all of these distinct actions are considered together, the results of this discussion can be reduced to quite simple terms—*C* over *B*, *B* over *A*, and hence *C* over *A*. Since the relationship is transitive, *C* must be preferred prima facie to *A* in any action between them. The equities seem correct, because *C* did nothing at all; *B* hit *C*; and *A* compelled *B* to so act.

The argument developed in trespass and extended to assault applies with equal force here, once the expanded, nonreciprocal notion of causation is accepted. In each two-party situation, one person must win and the other lose, while the rights and duties of third parties need not be taken into account until raised in suits in which they participate. With this kind of scheme, the question of "who is responsible" must be settled between the parties to the lawsuit. And again, it is the notion of causation that prima facie provides the answer.

Causation and Dangerous Conditions. The forms of causation thus far developed are the easiest to comprehend and accept. But an analysis of causation is seriously incomplete if made only in terms of force, fright, and compulsion. Both ordinary thought and legal theory also use a causal paradigm which covers cases involving the creation of dangerous conditions that result in harm to either person or property.

This paradigm shares many of the characteristics of the three paradigms already considered. Although it includes both cases where the dangerous condition is created by human acts and those where it is the result of natural events, the defendant's responsibility depends on a showing that *he* created the dangerous condition in question. The concept of volition thus remains necessary to mark off the class of human acts from the class of natural events. Moreover, the arguments on the question of responsibility parallel those already developed. *A* created the dangerous condition that resulted in harm to *B*; *B* did not create the dangerous condition that resulted in harm to *A*. The initial balance between the parties is upset, here as before, in a manner which links the parties to each other as it differentiates their roles.

But there are significant differences between this paradigm and those that have come before. First, it makes use of the expression, "result in." While it could be objected that this term defines causation in terms of itself, that is not the case. The term "result in" is intended to cover only those cases of causation—force, fright, and compulsion—already developed in previous chapters. In each individual case, it can, and must, be replaced with a description of the particular act or event which is the immediate cause of the harm, where the term "immediate" is used in its literal sense. The creation of a dangerous condition, without more, does not cause harm in the narrow sense of the term. Some further act or event of the kinds already considered must be identified before the causal analysis is completed, and the term "results in" calls attention to that fact. In effect, therefore, this paradigm, unlike those that preceded it, will require a detailed examination of these subsequent acts and events under a wide range of circumstances and conditions.

Second, this paradigm applies only to dangerous conditions. It is possible to divide the most common instances of dangerous conditions into three classes.[51] The first includes things that are "inherently" dangerous, of which stored explosives are the most common example. They are inherently dangerous because they retain their *potential* energy in full, even if they are stored or handled with the highest possible care.[52] A small application of force, or small change in conditions, like temperature and humidity, can release or otherwise set in motion large forces that can cause harm in the narrow sense of that term. The potential for danger remains great even if its probability is low.

The second kind of dangerous condition is created when a person places a thing—not dangerous in itself—in a dangerous position. Instances of this form of dangerous condition are of two sorts. The first class presupposes the recognition of rights of way: highways, footpaths, and the like. Thus, A leaves a roller skate in a walkway such that someone can slip and fall, should he step on it. Or B leaves his truck on the highway where it blocks or obstructs the road to oncoming traffic.

Other situations in this class involve any unstable position where the application of a small force will permit the release of

---

[51]The classification that follows was developed in John Charlesworth, Liability for Dangerous Things (1922).

[52]See discussion of Montgomery v. National C. & T. Co., 186 S.C. 167, 195 S.E. 247 (1937); pp. 53–55, *infra*.

some greater force. Here again, the term "unstable" is to be taken in its narrow physical sense. *C* places a large rock in an unstable position on top of a steep hillside where a light rain or the brush of a hand could send it tumbling to the base of the hill. *D* drops a vase, or places it on the edge of a table where it can be easily pulled to the ground by the force of gravity. *Vincent v. Lake Erie,* taken in its own terms, is a case of this sort: In the words of the court, "those in charge of the vessel deliberately and by their direct efforts held her in such a position that damage to the dock resulted."[53] The damage "resulted" not from gravity but "because of the wind and waves striking her starboard quarter with such force that she was constantly being lifted and thrown against the dock."

The third kind of dangerous situation concerns products or other things dangerous because defective. Thus, *E* fashions a chair that cannot support the weight of a 150-pound man because its legs are insecurely fastened to the seat; *F* manufactures a rifle with a weak barrel that can shatter when it is fired; or *G* constructs a lathe with inadequate screws to hold the wood in place when the lathe is in operation.[54] In each of these cases, the person who made the product has created a dangerous condition that causes harm when subjected to the stress that it was designed to receive when used in its intended manner. It is this concept of dangerous because defective that is crucial to the formulation of products liability rules (even when strict liability principles are not adopted), and the term here is used only in that standard sense.[55]

The use of this paradigm requires us to distinguish between these kinds of dangerous condition on the one hand and "mere" conditions on the other.[56] If all conditions, and not only danger-

---

[53]109 Minn. at 459, 124 N.W. at 222. The "deliberately" is in principle immaterial to the case given the theories of strict liability. 109 Minn. at 457–58, 124 N.W. at 221.

[54]Greenman v. Yuba Power Products, 59 Cal. 2d 57, 60, 377 P. 2d 897, 899 (1962).

[55]See Restatement of Torts 2d, § 402A.

[56]The distinction between types of dangerous conditions is immaterial for the development of the general theory, and probably is immaterial in the law today. Nevertheless, the distinction between things inherently dangerous and things dangerous because defective was important in the development of the law. In the effort to limit the effect of the privity requirement imposed in Winterbottom v. Wright, 10 M. & W. 109 (Exch. 1842) (itself an easy case for liability on the facts), it was early held that the privity limitation did not apply to products that were inherently dangerous when negligently labeled. Thomas v. Winchester, 6 N.Y. 396 (1852). Indeed in one sense McPherson v. Buick, 217 N.Y. 382, 111 N.E. 1050

ous ones, were given causal status, then in almost every case the conduct of both the plaintiff and the defendant would both be the "cause" of the harm in question, as a few examples help make plain. *H* leaves her carving knife in her kitchen drawer. A thief steals the knife and uses it to wound *I*. Has *H* caused *I* harm in any sense of the term? *J* leaves his car parked on the street. During the night a cyclone picks the car up and carries it along for a half-mile until it falls on top of *K*. Has *J* caused *K* harm? The answer to these questions is no. Unlike the cases of dangerous conditions above, neither *H* nor *J* could be sued on a theory which alleges that they created a dangerous condition that resulted in harm. It might be possible to show on the strength of other facts not present that these acts were dangerous when performed. But they are not dangerous as described, for in none of these cases did the prospective defendants make a store of energy which was released by the act of a third party or by natural events. It is also possible to state cases that are quite close to this line. The term "dangerous" has a residual vagueness that makes it difficult to apply in some instances.[57] But unless one is prepared to argue that these situations could not be distinguished from the three classes set out

---

(1916), stands, within the framework of the law of negligence, only for the proposition that neither things inherently dangerous, nor things dangerous because defective, are subject to the rule of Winterbottom v. Wright. Thus Cardozo states (217 N.Y. at 389, 111 N.E. at 1053): "We hold, then, that the principle of Thomas v. Winchester is not limited to poisons, explosives, and things of like nature, to things which in their normal operation are implements of destruction. . . . In this view of the defendant's liability there is nothing inconsistent with the theory of liability on which the case was tried. It is true that the court told the jury that 'an automobile is not an inherently dangerous vehicle.' The meaning, however, is made plain by the context. The meaning is that danger is not to be expected when the vehicle is well constructed. The court left it to the jury to say whether the defendant ought to have foreseen that the car, if negligently constructed, would become 'imminently dangerous.' Subtle distinctions are drawn by the defendant between things inherently dangerous and things imminently dangerous, but the case does not turn upon these verbal niceties. If danger was to be expected as reasonably certain, there was a duty of vigilance, and this whether you call the danger inherent or imminent."

[57]Indeed, Vincent v. Lake Erie would have been decided differently if the defendant's ship had been fastened to the dock with heavy rope, before the storm developed. The dissent makes a forceful point when it notes: "The reasoning of the opinion admits that if the ropes or cables, first attached to the dock had not parted, or if, in the first instance, the master had used the stronger cables, there would be no liability." 109 Minn. at 461, 124 N.W. at 222. See also the remarks of Lord MacMillan in Read v. Lyons, [1947] A.C. 156, 172-73.

above, then it must be accepted that there is some content to the term. Indeed, it seems idle to treat the concept as though it were immaterial, since it pervades the entire fabric of the law of tort.[58] The important question concerns its place in the scheme of liability.

The analysis of this last paradigm is not completed by proof that causal significance attaches only to dangerous conditions. It is also necessary to consider the kinds of acts and events that operate upon the condition so created to complete the causal chain. To consider the question of intermediate acts first, it is best to divide them into the three categories in which they are analyzed by Hart and Honoré: accidental, negligent, and deliberate.

Accidental acts cause little difficulty. On all views of the law, they do not break the causal connection between the plaintiff's injury and the defendant's conduct, whether performed by the plaintiff or a third party. Indeed, if they did not complete the causal link, then in effect no dangerous conditions could ever rise to causal significance. There could, for example, be no recovery in the simplest cases of products liability, because the very use of the defendant's product would serve on causal grounds to defeat an action for injuries sustained.

Again, the acts of either the plaintiff or a third party do not break the causal connection between the defendant's conduct and the plaintiff's harm, even if negligently performed. Negligence in this context means, as ever, the failure to take reasonable steps that could have prevented or avoided the harm in question. Since the forces attributable to the plaintiff or the third party operate on the dangerous condition created by the defendant, proof that either the plaintiff or a third party failed to exercise reasonable care does not deny the causal allegations contained in the prima facie case; it remains true that the dangerous condition created by the defendant resulted in the harm to the plaintiff. Force and dangerous conditions are still the only issues material to the causation question.

To make the discussion concrete, consider again the case where A slips and falls on a roller skate placed by B on the walkway. Even if it could be shown that A could have avoided the harm if

---

[58]Restatement of Torts § 519 (ultrahazardous activities); Restatement of Torts 2d, § 402 (defective products). See also W. T. S. Stallybrass, Dangerous Things and the Non-natural User of Land, 3 Camb. L.J. 376 (1929).

he had looked where he stepped, it is still the case that he slipped on the skate and fell: Only the act that created the dangerous condition and that which was the immediate cause of the harm need be taken into account to complete the causal description of the events in question. The requisites of this paradigm of causation—the slip and the fall—are met whether or not *A* was careless.

A's carelessness might be regarded as sufficient to support the defense of contributory negligence. The acceptance of contributory negligence as a defense is natural in a system that presupposes that the plaintiff must allege negligence in order to complete his prima facie case. But let the defendant's negligence be regarded as immaterial to the prima facie case, and it is then difficult to see why the plaintiff's negligence should raise a valid affirmative defense. All the objections to Hand's account of negligence and its place in the scheme of tort law apply with equal force to the defense of contributory negligence to the statement of the prima facie case. If notions of efficient resource allocation do not provide the proper measure of the defendant's conduct, they should not be introduced by the back door in the judgment of the plaintiff's conduct.

By like reasoning, if the act requirement is crucial in the statement of the prima facie case, it should be crucial as well in the analysis of any possible defenses. The plaintiff's act, reference to his want of precautions apart, does not, for the reasons just discussed in conjunction with the accidental conduct of the plaintiff, provide the basis for an affirmative defense. Hence the case for the defendant must rest upon his ability to demonstrate that the plaintiff owes him a duty at common law to take reasonable steps for self-protection, a question that is discussed at length in chapter IV. But even if such a duty is recognized, the point is that the allegation of carelessness by the plaintiff does not affect the judgment that the conduct of the defendant was, under the paradigm of dangerous conditions, the cause of the harm in question.

It remains only to examine the causal connection between the dangerous condition created by the defendant and the harm to the plaintiff in the most difficult case, where the intermediate actor deliberately inflicted the harm in question. In *Causation in the Law*, Hart and Honoré argue that it is not possible to establish causal antecedents to a deliberate act designed to inflict harm. On their view, one could never hold responsible a person who creates a dangerous condition of which the intermediate actor takes advantage out of his own desire to inflict the harm. "The general principle of the traditional doctrine is that *the free, deliberate and informed act or omission of a human being, intended to produce the consequence which is in fact produced, negatives causal connexion.*"[59] In support of this "common sense" position, they argue that "voluntary acts" (deliberate acts where neither mistake nor coercion is present) enjoy a special status because "precautions against such acts are specially difficult, since a man who is bent on harm will usually find some way of doing it."[60]

The case appears to be overstated. It does not follow, because a man bent upon harm *usually* can find some way of doing it, that one must *never* seek to go behind a deliberate infliction of harm. There are many cases where the harm, even if deliberate, could be inflicted only because of the dangerous condition created by the defendant. For example, assume that the defendant has placed a boulder perilously close to the edge of a ravine. One day when the plaintiff is in the ravine—it matters not why—*X*, his bitter enemy, sees him from the side of the ravine and, bent upon his destruction, tips the boulder over the side of the ravine where it falls

---

[59]H. L. A. Hart & A. M. Honoré, *supra* note 6, at 129. Note that Hart and Honoré argue that the same principle applies to both acts and omissions. But the cases cannot be regarded as parallel after they are placed in the framework of the causal paradigms already developed. If *X* deliberately chooses not to prevent *A* from hitting *B* when he is able to do so, *B* still has an action against *A* of the form "*A* hit *B*." But that action will not be open to *B* where the act of *X* is the immediate cause of the harm. *X* hit *B*, not *A*. Hence if *B* is to have any case in tort against *A* it must come to grips with the paradigm of dangerous conditions. Where *A* hits *B*, *B* must then come to grips with the good Samaritan problem, discussed in chap. IV, in order to maintain his action against *X*.

[60]*Id.* at 129. There is one exception to the general rule: "Where it is clear that the ground for regarding conduct as negligent, or the reason for prohibiting it by rule, is the very fact that it provides an opportunity, commonly exploited by others, for deliberate wrongdoing, it would obviously be senseless to treat their voluntary intervention as a ground for relieving the person who has provided the opportunity for it of the responsibility for the harm which they have done." *Id.* at 6. This class of events extends the notion of causation to its outer limits because it insists that a condition by the defendant be regarded as dangerous because it exposes the plaintiff or his property to the risk of deliberate harm inflicted by a third party. There is much sense in this position, because it is quite likely that a thief will steal goods from a stand or a cart that has been, say, overturned which he would not and could not steal if the confusion had not been created. See, *e.g.,* Brower v. New York Central R.R., 91 N.J.L. 190, 103 A. 166 (1918), where a sharply divided court held the defendant liable.

upon the plaintiff, severely injuring him. X, even if bent upon destruction, took advantage of the dangerous condition created by the defendant, especially if X had no alternative means at his disposal to execute his plans. If alternative means were available, the defendant should be required to prove the fact as an affirmative defense to the cause of action.[61] Such proof does not deny the causal allegations contained in the prima facie case, but only shows that they do not, in the circumstances, support the claim to relief. The issues of causation and responsibility should be kept distinct. The relationship between them is not clarified by the invocation of a per se rule that states that the causal connection is severed wherever a third party seizes upon the dangerous situation so created in order to deliberately inflict harm. The intent of X should be of no concern in the action between the plaintiff and the defendant. Its role, if any, is to ensure that the defendant should have an action over against X if he should be able to find him.

Nonetheless, cases of the deliberate infliction of harm by an intervening action do raise particularly difficult problems of proof, because there will be many situations where the third party will not seize upon the dangerous *aspects* of the situation created by the defendant. For example, assume that the defendant leaves a vase precariously perched on the edge of a high shelf. Y picks up that vase and throws it upon the head of the plaintiff who was sitting in a position where he could have been struck by the vase if it had fallen. Here the defendant is not liable because there is no causal connection between his conduct and the plaintiff's harm. Y could have caused the same destruction even if that vase had been placed in a safe and stable position in the middle of the shelf. The dangerous potential in the antecedent situation did not "result in" harm to the plaintiff. In cases like these Hart and Honoré are correct, but it is improper to generalize from them to the broad proposition that it is never proper in a causal sense to go behind the deliberate act of a third person.[62]

[61]See Mayor of New York v. Lord, 18 Wend. 126, 130 (N.Y. Sup. Ct. 1837).

[62]The position of the Restatement has this in common with the argument in the text: It holds that the intervening act of a third person breaks the causal connection in only some cases. Nevertheless, it falls back upon the distinction between "foreseeable" and "unforeseeable" intervening acts as the means to decide particular cases, Restatement of Torts 2d, § 442(B) & comment c at 471 (1965). But given the analysis in the text, it is possible to handle these questions without reference to the concept of foresight and its attendant difficulties.

Thus far we have considered the effects that intervening acts have on the causal connection between the dangerous condition created by the defendant and the harm suffered by the plaintiff. A similar analysis applies when we consider the effect of intervening events. In *Causation in the Law,* Hart and Honoré divide forces of nature essentially into "big" and "little" forces.[63] In their view, the little forces never break the chain of causation; when operative they serve only to complete it.[64] That position has received general acceptance, and for the same reason that accidental acts never serve to negate the causal connection. If these forces of nature broke the causal connection, then the concept of causation would have to be restricted to cases of trespass, assault, and compulsion; dangerous conditions would have no role in causal analysis.

But the other portion of their argument, which holds that *vis major* or other "abnormal events" serve to break the causal connection, does not appear to be correct in all circumstances. Here the argument is the same as in the case of intervening acts designed to inflict deliberate harm. In some cases forces of nature, no matter how great, can operate only upon the antecedent dangerous conditions created by the defendant. For example, if a huge storm pushes the boulder off the edge of a cliff when a gentle rain could have had the same effect, it is hard to see why the storm should break the causal connection that would otherwise have been completed by the breeze. Here the large force, like the small one, only places the boulder in a position where it could be pulled downward by the force of gravity. The storm did not hurl the boulder onto the plaintiff. Again, the gale winds in *Vincent* did not break the causal connection (and no one even suggested it did) when the

---

[63] H. L. A. Hart & A. M. Honoré, *supra* note 6, at 31–38, 152–53. Hart and Honoré do not single out the forces of nature for separate consideration. But to the extent that the distinction between "normal" and "abnormal" conditions applies to them, the uncertain line is between "big" and "little" forces.

[64] "Thus if X lights a fire in the open and, shortly after, a normal gentle breeze gets up and the fire spreads to Y's property, X's action is the cause of the harm, though without the subsequent breeze no harm would have occurred; the bare fact that the breeze was subsequent to X's action (and also causally independent of it) does not destroy its status as a mere condition or make it a 'superseding' cause. To achieve the latter status, a subsequent occurrence must at least have some characteristic by which common sense usually distinguishes causes from mere conditions." H. L. A. Hart & A. M. Honoré, *supra* note 6, at 36.

defendant continued to hold its ship firm in a position when the winds would dash it against the dock.

Nonetheless, the distinction between large forces and small ones does have importance, because the larger the force, the greater the probability that the defendant did not create a dangerous condition upon which the force acted, and the easier to accept the assertion that the force of nature accomplished all of its destruction on its own without operating upon a dangerous condition created by defendant. For example, if the defendant leaves his automobile atop a hill with its brakes released and its wheels away from the curb, the position of the car, although dangerous, would be quite immaterial if a cyclone lifted the car and carried it a great distance until it landed upon the plaintiff's house. Here the proof of those events shows, as with the case of deliberate harms, that the antecedent dangerous condition bore no causal relationship to the harm.

The theory of causation just developed—that of dangerous conditions—must in all its aspects be distinguished carefully from the "but for" analysis of causation rejected earlier. When a "but for" theory of causation is adopted, the proposition in question takes the form, "but for the negligence (or act) of the defendant, the harm to the plaintiff would never have occurred." That proposition is, to repeat, counterfactual in form, and thus differs linguistically from the assertion, just made, of the form: "The dangerous conditions created by the defendant resulted in harm to the plaintiff," where the proposition remains in the indicative mood throughout, with its emphasis upon what the defendant *did*. The verb "resulted in" covers only the specific kinds of causes discussed in the previous paradigms. Its use does not suggest that the consequences of a given act may extend indefinitely.

A series of examples should clarify both the similarities and differences between the two theories. *A* digs a hole in a public highway which is a menace to all traffic that uses it. *B*, even several days later, rides along that highway and is thrown from his car when he drives into that hole. He should be able to maintain his prima facie case against *A* on the ground that *A* created the dangerous condition that resulted in *B*'s harm, even though *B* had to drive his car into the hole in order to complete the causal connection. Similarly, if *B* lost control of his car and hit *C*, then *C* should have an action against *A* as well. Thus far, there is no distinction between the results under the two theories because one could say with equal force that but for the fact that A dug the hole in the highway, the injuries to B or C would never have happened. But there are instances where a person would escape liability on the causal principles developed here even if his conduct was judged the cause of injuries under the "but for" test. Assume, for example, that when A dug his hole in the highway, it was immediately brought to the attention of the public authorities, who sent D out to repair the road. Assume further that, after he completed the job, D struck E at an intersection when he ran the light in an effort to get home in time for an early dinner. On these facts, the but-for analysis would hold that A (or his negligence) was the "cause" of the harm in question, even if not its only cause. It is true that A might not be held liable for the injuries that occurred, but this would require the invocation of some ad hoc limitation upon causation based upon a notion of foresight or duty. In many cases those tests will achieve only the results which follow from theories of causation that reject "but for" doctrines. In those circumstances they are inelegant but harmless. In others, like *Bolton v. Stone,* their use is fatal. Once the concept of causation is limited to dangerous conditions that release or otherwise redirect forces in the narrowest sense of causation, it is clear that there is no causal connection between A's act of digging the hole and the subsequent injuries to B. No one tripped, fell, or drove into the hole, or even swerved to avoid it. The causal connection ends once the road is repaired, regardless of the results that would follow from the use of the "but for" theories.

It can also be shown that this account of causation is consistent with the rules of strict liability. It is true that the term "dangerous" often carries with it suggestions of both the degree of risk and the probability of harm, but in the restricted sense the term is used here—with the emphasis upon the "potential" to cause harm in the narrow sense of that term—more than a verbal mutation is at stake. The law of negligence, as expressed in the formula of Learned Hand, requires balancing the risk and probable extent of harm against the burden of the costs needed either to eliminate or reduce it. No cost-benefit analysis is required, however, when the theories of dangerous conditions are used to establish the causal connection between the defendant's conduct and the plaintiff's harm. It could well be that the defendant acts in a reasonable

45

manner when he creates a dangerous condition that results in harm to the plaintiff. It may not be worthwhile for him to see that all of his manufactured products are free from defects; but nonetheless he will be held liable if any of them should prove defective and cause harm.

Again, take the case of a defendant who digs a hole in a back road because he is made to do so at gunpoint. Here the use of a cost-benefit analysis suggests that the expected harm of the activity is much less than the expected harm of the alternative. Moreover, the specific defense of compulsion by a third person should be available to the defendant under the standard negligence theories. Nonetheless, a given plaintiff who is injured when he falls into that hole should be able, prima facie, to recover from the defendant on the theories of causation developed here. The compulsion by the third party has precisely the same effect that it has in the trespass cases. It supports the defendant's (ordinarily futile) action over against the gunman, should he be sued by the plaintiff. It also supports the plaintiff's direct action against the gunman, the latter action taking the form that the gunman compelled another person to dig a hole in the highway into which the plaintiff fell (which resulted in his injury). But it is not a defense in the immediate action.

The parallels to the trespass cases can be extended. If the defendant dug the hole in an effort to find water to quench his thirst, then the action would still be allowed, because the defense of private necessity is inapplicable here as in trespass cases. The rules of causation based upon the paradigm of a dangerous condition differ from the rules of negligence because they do not permit the defenses of either compulsion by a third party or private necessity. In all these cases, the defendant created a dangerous condition even though he acted as a reasonable man. The dangerous condition is only the causal substitute for the force required in the trespass cases. Otherwise, the pattern of argumentation in the two theories remains precisely the same.

But even though all these theories of causation are theories of strict liability, there are differences between them. The prima facie cases of trespass and assault turned on (in addition to "volition") only notions of force and fright. Mention of "dangerous" activities in trespass cases does not serve to explicate the concept of causation. The "force" applied by the defendant makes the concept nonreciprocal; the concept of "dangerous" need not be invoked for that end. Its use in the trespass context as an equivalent to "risky" only adds an additional substantive requirement, much akin to negligence, to the prima facie case. *A* hit *B* could not set up the prima facie case if it had to be shown that *A*'s activities were dangerous. Once the trespass actions are put to one side and attention is turned to the causal significance of conditions, the term "dangerous" no longer functions as a substitute for "risky," no longer functions as a separate substantive requirement. Instead, in each of its senses it becomes part and parcel of the extended notion of causation which requires us to take into account at least one further act or event in order to explain the harm in question.

The distinction between the kinds of causation is thus crucial to the development of the law. Moreover, its importance was recognized in imperfect form at common law. During the years that the forms of action controlled, English lawyers drew the distinction between trespass and trespass on the case. Each of these actions was governed by its own writ, and in the early stages at least case could lie only if trespass did not. The mistake of the common lawyers lay not in their recognition of the distinction between the forms of action, but in their insistence that trespass actions (where the causal link is clear) were actions of strict liability, while actions on the case for "indirect" harm required proof of negligence or intent.[65] That distinction makes no more sense than the modern rules which hold that automobile accidents (usually collision cases) are governed by negligence principles while products liability cases (which are never trespass cases) are governed by the principles of strict liability. Both kinds of cases are governed by strict liability principles, once the causation rules are well developed. The line between trespass and case, stated at common law and implicitly followed today, is crucial only on the question whether the causal paradigm of force or that of dangerous conditions is applicable to the case. "The forms of action we have buried, but they still rule us from their graves."[66]

The rules of liability thus far developed have not relied upon

---

[65]See generally C. H. S. Fifoot, History and Sources of the Common Law 66–73 (1949); O. W. Holmes, Jr., The Common Law 90 (1881).

[66]F. W. Maitland, The Forms of Action at Common Law 2 (1936 ed.).

any form of cost-benefit analysis. But even though they have not sought to take into account any economic principles, it does not follow that they must offend them. Consider the two most difficult cases—simple accident and necessity—that could arise under any of these causal paradigms. In both these cases the rules imposing liability upon the defendant should not in principle create any new incentives, once it is settled that the plaintiff's conduct is not in issue. For example, in *Bolton v. Stone* the defendant will not take any precautions, because it is cheaper to satisfy the judgment if the accident should occur. There is no question of resource allocation. There is only the question whether the courts will compel the transfer of wealth from one person to another, and on that issue it seems appropriate that the decision should be made on grounds of fairness.

The same analysis applies to the case of necessity. Defendants in cases like *Vincent* will be required to make compensation for avoidable damages, regardless of the theory of recovery invoked. The theories of strict liability diverge from those of negligence only with regard to that portion of the damages against which no prudent precautions could have been taken. As to these the economic situation is exactly what it was in *Bolton v. Stone*; it will be cheaper for the defendant to pay the damages than to take the precautions, so the precautions will not be taken. There is still no question of resource allocation, and as before, it is appropriate to rely upon fairness grounds in order to decide whether the transfer payment will be required.

Finally, it can be argued that rules of strict liability are in the end preferable on economic grounds because they reduce the administrative costs of decision. The point is clear in cases like *Vincent* because rules of strict liability eliminate the need to allocate between recoverable and nonrecoverable damages. But, more important, the rules of strict liability tell the courts that they need not take into account any form of economic analysis in order to decide the concrete case. There is no need to ask the hard question of which branch of government is best able to make cost-benefit determinations, because the matter is left in private hands where it belongs. It is true that the rules of strict liability may in the aggregate lead to some small increase in the number of cases to be decided by the courts, but even that is doubtful since it is so simple for plaintiffs to include some allegation of negligence in their complaint in order to state a prima facie case.

Nor need the point be left only to theoretical speculation. In this context it is interesting to note the observations that sociologist H. Laurence Ross makes about the methods which insurance adjusters use to settle cases under the "fault" system:

> The formal law of negligence liability, as stated in casebooks from the opinions of appellate courts, is not easily applied to the accident at Second and Main. It deals with violation of a duty of care owed by the insured to the claimant and is based on a very complex and perplexing model of the "reasonable man," in this case the reasonable driver. . . . In their day-to-day work, the concern with liability is reduced to the question of whether either or both parties violated the rules of the road as expressed in common traffic laws. Taking the doctrine of negligence *per se* to an extreme doubtless unforeseen by the makers of the formal law, adjusters tend to define a claim as one of liability or of no liability depending only on whether a rule was violated, regardless of intention, knowledge, necessity, and other such qualifications that might receive sympathetic attention even from a traffic court judge. Such a determination is far easier than the task proposed in theory by the formal law of negligence.
>
> To illustrate, if Car A strikes Car B from the rear, the driver of A is assumed to be liable and B is not. In the ordinary course of events, particularly where damages are routine, the adjuster is not concerned with *why* A struck B, or with whether A violated a duty of care to B, or with whether A was unreasonable or not. These questions are avoided, not only because they may be impossible to answer, but also because the fact that A struck B from the rear will satisfy all supervisory levels that a payment is in order, without further explanation. Likewise, in the routine case, the fact that A was emerging from a street governed by a stop sign will justify treating this as a case of liability, without concern for whether the sign was seen or not, whether there was adequate reason for not seeing the sign, etc. In short, in the ordinary case the physical facts of the accident are normally sufficient to allocate liability between the drivers. Inasmuch as the basic physical facts of the accident are easily known—and they are frequently ascertainable from the first notice—the issue of liability is usually relatively easy to dispose of.[67]

The cleavage between the appellate rules and the daily practices is sharp and clear. There is abundant theoretical support, however, for the common sense rules of thumb adopted in the daily resolution of accident cases. Here is one case where the theories of law should be changed to conform to the common practice.

[67]H. Laurence Ross, Settled Out of Court—The Social Process of Insurance Claims Adjustment 98–99 (1970).

IV. The Problem of the Good Samaritan

Chapters II and III have compared the common law rules of negligence with those of strict liability in cases where the defendant has harmed the plaintiff's person or property. If that analysis is sound, then the rules of liability should be based upon the harm in fact caused and not upon any subsequent determination of the reasonableness of the defendant's conduct. The question of liability is thereby severed from both general cost-benefit analysis of the defendant's conduct and a moral examination of his individual worth. In the cases of affirmative action, the rules of strict liability avoid both the unfairness and complications created when negligence, in either its economic or moral sense, is accepted as the basis of the tort law.

The purpose of this chapter is to show that these conclusions are capable of extension to areas in which the law has traditionally not allowed recovery. The theories of strict liability explain and justify, as the rules of reasonableness cannot, the common law's refusal to extend liability in tort to cases where the defendant has not harmed the plaintiff by his affirmative action.[1] The problem arises in its starkest form in the case of the good Samaritan. A finds himself in a perilous situation which was not created by B, as when A is overwhelmed by cramps while swimming alone in a surging sea. B, moreover, is in a position where he could, without any danger of injury to himself, come to A's assistance with some simple and well-nigh costless steps, such as throwing a rope to the plaintiff. The traditional common law position has been that there is no cause of action against B solely because B, in effect, permitted A to drown.

It is important to note the manner in which such cases should

---

[1] I put aside here all those cases in which there are special relationships between the plaintiff and the defendants: parent and child, invitor and invitee, and the like.

be decided under a negligence system. In the verbal formulation of the law of negligence, little attention is paid to the distinction between those cases in which the defendant acted and those cases in which he did not act, failed to act, or omitted to act. "Negligence is the *omission* to do something which a reasonable man guided upon those considerations which ordinarily regulate the conduct of human affairs, would do, or doing something which a prudent and reasonable man would not do."[2] The distinction between acts and omissions is of no consequence to the economic analysis of negligence contained in cases like *Carroll Towing*, for there the emphasis is placed in part upon those precautions which a defendant should have taken (but did not take) in order to prevent those instrumentalities which he owns (here the boat in the harbor) from causing harm to other persons.

Thus, if one considers the low costs of prevention to *B* of rescuing *A*, and the serious, if not deadly, harm that *A* will suffer if *B* chooses not to rescue him, there is no reason why the *Carroll Towing* formula or the general rules of negligence should not require, under pain of liability, the defendant to come to the aid of the plaintiff. Nonetheless, the good Samaritan problem receives special treatment even under the modern law of torts. The reasons for the special position of this problem are clear once the theories of strict liability are systematically applied. Under these rules, the act requirement has to be satisfied in order to show that the defendant in a given lawsuit caused harm to the plaintiff. Once that is done, the private predicament of the defendant, his ability to take precautions against the given risk, and the general economic rationality of his conduct are all beside the point.[3] Only the issue of causation, of what *the defendant did*, is material to the statement of the prima facie case. The theory is not utilitarian.[4] It looks not

---

[2]Blyth v. Birmingham Waterworks, 11 Exch. 781, 784, 156 Eng. Rep. 1047, 1049 (1856) (emphasis added).

[3]Whatever the historical motivation behind the rule, its validity does not rest on the assumption that "the individual [is] competent to protect himself if not interfered with from without." Francis H. Bohlen, Studies in the Law of Torts 295 (1926). If that were the basis of the rule, it could not apply to infants or lunatics about whom the assumption of "competence" has never been made.

[4]But see James Barr Ames, Law and Morals, *supra* chap. II, note 3, at 110: "The law is utilitarian. It exists for the realization of the reasonable needs of the community. If the interest of an individual runs counter to this chief object of the law, it must be sacrificed."

to the consequences of alternate course of conduct but to what was done. When that theory with its justification is applied to the problem of the good Samaritan, it follows in the case just put that *A* should not be able to recover from *B* for his injuries. No matter how the facts are manipulated, it is not possible to argue that *B* caused *A* harm in any of the senses of causation which were developed in the earlier portions of this article when he failed to render assistance to *A* in his time of need. In typical negligence cases, all the talk of avoidance and reasonable care may shift attention from the causation requirement, which the general "but for" test distorts beyond recognition. But its importance is revealed by its absence in the good Samaritan cases where the presence of all those elements immaterial to tortious liability cannot, even in combination, persuade judges who accept the negligence theory to apply it in the decisive case.

The principles of strict liability do more than explain the reasons behind the general common law refusal to require men to be good Samaritans. They also explain why it is that in some cases there are strong arguments to support apparent exceptions to the common law position. The point is best illustrated by two cases. The first case is put by Ames:

> We may suppose again that the situation of imminent danger of death was created by the act, but the innocent act, of the person who refuses to prevent the death. The man, for example, whose eye was penetrated by the glancing shot of the careful pheasant hunter, stunned by the shot, fell face downward into a shallow pool by which he was standing. The hunter might easily save him, but lets him drown.[5]

The second situation, that of *Montgomery v. National C. & T.,* is described by Gregory as follows:

> Consider this situation. Two of defendant's trucks, due to no fault of the drivers, became stalled on a narrow road, completely blocking the highway. Also, without fault, the men were unable to get the trucks started again. This was at the foot of a short hill, which obscured the view of approaching drivers. Moreover, the hill was somewhat icy. Plaintiff came driving along at a normal speed. By the time he saw the stalled trucks, he was unable to stop and crashed

[5]James Barr Ames, *supra* chap. II, note 3, at 112.

into them. Had one of defendant's truck drivers climbed the hill and posted a warning, this accident would not have happened.[6]

The first of these cases was not the subject of a judicial decision, but Ames was of the opinion that under the modern law "a lawyer who should try to charge the hunter would lead a forlorn hope," because the defendant "simply failed to confer a benefit upon a stranger.[7] In the second case, however, the South Carolina court found that the defendant could be held liable on account of the actionable negligence of its employees in the course of their employment, because on the facts of the case the employees had both the opportunity and the means to place warnings in some form at the top of the hill which would have enabled the plaintiff to avoid the crash in question. The court insisted that this duty rested upon the defendant's employees even though two propositions are settled: first, that no passerby would have been charged with that duty, even if he had the time and means to have taken those steps; and second, that the defendant's employees would have been under no duty to place those warnings if the road had been blocked, say, by a falling tree.[8] In effect, the position of the court is that simply because the defendant's employees blocked the road, they were under a duty to take those precautions reasonably calculated to prevent possible injury to other users of the highway.

Under the theories of strict liability neither of these defendants could take advantage of the good Samaritan doctrine. The hunter should be liable in a trespass action because he shot the plaintiff. Once negligence is no longer regarded as the lynchpin of the law, it should not matter that after the shooting the defendant was in a position to give aid to the plaintiff. He would be held liable even if he were not. The case no longer raises the problem of the good Samaritan; it is a simple case of trespass governed by the rules of strict liability set out above.

The second case is subject to a similar analysis, only here the appropriate theory of causation is the theory of dangerous conditions. The defendant is liable because harm resulted when the

---

[6]Charles O. Gregory, The Good Samaritan and the Bad, in The Good Samaritan and the Law 22, 27 (James Ratcliffe ed. 1966).

[7]James Barr Ames, *supra* chap. II, note 3, at 113, 112.

[8]Charles O. Gregory, *supra* note 6, at 27.

plaintiff's car ran into its truck after his employees blocked the road. It is immaterial that the defendant's employees had an opportunity to place warnings at the top of the hill, because the theory of dangerous conditions, too, is a theory of strict liability. Once it is shown that the plaintiff's conduct (he hit the defendant's truck) only serves to complete the prima facie case, the liability follows, because the facts do not even suggest the basis for an affirmative defense.[9]

Theories of strict liability, therefore, support the results in both these cases in a simple and direct fashion. But it is not clear that these results are correct under a system of negligence which accepts as one of its premises that a man is under no duty to confer aid upon a stranger. In both these cases, the claim for liability is based upon the assumption that the defendant's conduct, although insufficient to create a prima facie case, is nonetheless sufficient to create some duty of care. Once created, each of these cases is to be treated as though it were a typical negligence case in which the defendant is under a duty to take reasonable steps to aid the plaintiff.

At common law, as Ames acknowledges, the "hunter" would have been liable "simply because he shot the other."[10] But if that allegation fails to state a prima facie case (or in the alternative is subject to the affirmative defense that the defendant was not negligent),[11] then it has been decided that the defendant should not be responsible for the harm to the plaintiff, even though he has caused it. On what grounds, therefore, can it be argued that the trespass does not create a prima facie case, but does create an affirmative duty of care? In his attack upon the rules of strict liability, Holmes argued that to hold a man liable only because he has harmed someone else is little better than to compel him to insure his neighbor against lightning.[12] If Holmes is correct, then it

---

[9]If the owner of the truck brought an action against the driver, claiming as its prima facie case, "you struck my truck," that action would fail because the defendant could plead as its affirmative defense, "you (plaintiff) blocked my right of way." Observe that there is no appeal here to a notion of contributory negligence, even though the defense puts plaintiff's conduct into issue.

[10]James Barr Ames, *supra* chap. II, note 3, at 113.

[11]It is odd that the assertion "The defendant was not negligent" would be treated as an *affirmative* defense.

[12]O. W. Holmes, Jr., *supra* chap. II, note 4, at 96.

follows that the defendant in the hunting case should be subjected to no additional burden because he shot the stranger. The conclusion is inescapable once accidental harms caused by the defendant are treated on a par with acts of God.

These arguments apply with equal force to *Montgomery v. National C. & T.* Defendant's drivers would have been under no duty to warn oncoming vehicles of the possible danger if the road had been blocked by a falling tree. Once it is accepted that an allegation that the defendant blocked the highway does not create a prima facie case, then, as in Ames's case, it seems improper to take refuge in a halfway house which says that the conduct of the defendant is nonetheless sufficient to obligate him to take reasonable steps for the benefit of the plaintiff. Again the act of the defendant must be treated like an act of God whether the issue is immediate liability or the recognition of a duty of care.

These variations on the good Samaritan rule illustrate the evasive responses that courts are prepared to make in order to restrict a rule that they accept but do not like. The point of the above discussion is that in some cases adoption of the theories of strict liability will reduce the potential scope of the good Samaritan problem because the cases will be governed by one of the causation paradigms set out in chapter III. But in a closely related context, the theories of strict liability will not work to expand liability. Assume that the defendant has caused harm to the plaintiff for which he is not liable solely because he has open to him a good affirmative defense, such as contributory negligence. The Restatement of Torts, for example, states that the defendant, although not liable for the initial injuries, is under a duty to render aid to the plaintiff.[13] In effect, this position holds that conduct insufficient to create liability may nonetheless call forth a duty of care. But once it is accepted that the defendant was not responsible for the harm he caused, then he should be able to treat the plaintiff as though he were a stranger who placed himself in a position of danger. At that point the general common law position on the good Samaritan question should govern, for the availability of a good defense eliminates the force of the prima facie case. The defendant could, if he chose, render him assistance, but should not be under obligation to do so.

---

[13]Restatement of Torts § 322. Contributory negligence is taken as a good defense only for the purposes of this argument.

There is a further class of exceptions to the good Samaritan rule, motivated by the same judicial distaste for the doctrine, which also cannot be rationalized by an appeal to the theories of strict liability. Consider the case where the defendant gratuitously takes steps to aid the plaintiff only to discontinue his efforts before the plaintiff is moved to a position of comparative safety. For example, A sees B lying unconscious on the public street. Immediately, he runs to the phone, dials an emergency room, and then hangs up the receiver. Or, in the alternative, he picks B up and places him in his automobile, only to return him to his original position on the sidewalk when he thinks, for whatever reason, better of the involvement.

It has often been argued that the good Samaritan doctrine in these situations is of no application on the ground that once the defendant undertakes to assist the plaintiff in distress, he can no longer claim that his conduct amounted to a "simple nonfeasance," no longer maintain that the two were still strangers in the eyes of the law. The general refusal of the law to require one man to come to aid another is only a consequence of the act requirement in the law of tort. But once the defendant dials the phone or moves the plaintiff, the act requirement is satisfied; and once satisfied, the defendant cannot disregard the welfare of a plaintiff whom he has taken into his charge.

This position must be rejected. The act requirement in the law of tort is but a combination of the volition and the causation requirements already discussed. The law of tort cannot be invoked simply because the defendant has done something; it must be shown that the act in question has caused harm to the plaintiff. Where the defendant has dialed the phone only to put the receiver back on the hook, he has acted, but those acts have not caused harm. The theories of force, fright, compulsion and dangerous condition are inapplicable, either alone or in combination, to the facts as described. The same result applies even where the defendant has moved the plaintiff's body. It is true that there is a technical trespass in that case, but unless it could be shown that the plaintiff was worse off afterward because he was moved, the causation requirement has not been satisfied even if there was more than simple nonfeasance by the plaintiff.

Properly conceived, these situations should be discussed together with other forms of gratuitous undertakings and the obligations they generate. The common law has never found a home for such obligations. They should not be part of the law of tort because they do not satisfy the causation requirement; and the unfortunate doctrine of consideration prevents their easy inclusion in the law of contracts. But even though the obligations attached to gratuitous undertakings stand in need of systematic examination, it is still in general the case that a defendant should not be compelled to complete a gratuitous undertaking against his will even where he has made an express promise to do so. And that result applies even if the defendant has taken steps to discharge his promise. A bare promise to pay $1000 does not become enforceable simply because the plaintiff has written a check for that amount; delivery is still required. Nor does the payment of $100 as the first of ten gratuitous installments obligate the donor to pay the other $900. In the case just put where the plaintiff is unconscious, there cannot of course be any question of an express promise. But it is only appropriate to hold that once a defendant begins to help a plaintiff in distress, he should be in no worse a position than a defendant who had made an express promise to assist. Even if the defendant has been of a partial assistance to the plaintiff, that does not of itself obligate the defendant to provide him with still further benefits. It follows that the defendant can discontinue his efforts at will and escape all liability unless he has caused harm to the plaintiff in one of the senses developed above.[14]

The same issue involved in the good Samaritan problem frequently arises when it is the *defendant* who claims in effect that the plaintiff was under an affirmative duty to take steps for his, the defendant's, benefit. The point is most clearly raised in connection with the maxim that a tortfeasor takes his victim as he finds him. The maxim applies where the defendant has tortiously harmed the plaintiff, and the issue is whether the latter is entitled to recover for those injuries which would not have occurred had the plaintiff had, in all material respects, a "normal" constitution.

[14]The hardest case of this sort arises where the defendant places the plaintiff in a position where he is no longer able to get help from others who might wish to aid him. Under those circumstances it is proper to hold the defendant liable, even though it is difficult to establish whether the help from some third party would indeed be forthcoming. See Zelenko v. Gimbel Bros., 158 Misc. 904, 287 N.Y. S. 134 (Sup. Ct. 1935). "Defendant *segregated* this plaintiff's intestate where such aid

The situation is illustrated by the facts of *Vosburg v. Putney.*[15]
The plaintiff was suffering from the aftereffects of a prior injury
to his leg. The defendant kicked the leg at its sore point and caused
a serious inflammation. Little or no harm would have been done
to an individual with a sound leg. Once it is accepted that the
plaintiff has a prima facie case against the defendant, whether on
a theory of strict liability, negligence, or "wrongful" intent,[16] the
question arises whether the plaintiff should be able to recover for
that portion of the damages that would not have been suffered by
a plaintiff with a healthy constitution. If he takes no precautions
to protect his knee, it should be possible for the defendant to
argue that the plaintiff's negligence bars his recovery if the
Carroll Towing formula is used to determine the reasonableness
of the plaintiff's conduct.[17] It could well be argued that, as be-

could not be given and then left her alone." *Id.* at 905, 287 N.Y.S. 135 (emphasis
added). The act requirement is satisfied in this statement of the cause of action.
[15]80 Wis. 523, 50 N.W. 403 (1891). *Vosburg* is not a clean case on its facts. Given
that the incident took place in the classroom, there are overtones of assumption of
risk which are not present in a case like Bolton v. Stone. Indeed the maxim, you
take your victim as you find him, would have found its clearest application in a
case like Bolton v. Stone if Miss Stone had had an unusually thin skull. Note,
moreover, that if assumption of risk could be proved in Vosburg v. Putney, it
would apply whether or not the plaintiff had a sore knee.
[16]The language in Vosburg v. Putney on the wrongful intent question is incom-
prehensible: "But this is an action to recover damages for an alleged assault and
battery. In such case the rule is correctly stated, in many of the authorities cited by
counsel, that plaintiff must show either that the intention was unlawful, or that the
defendant is in fault. If the intended act is unlawful, the intention to commit it
must necessarily be unlawful. Hence, as applied to this case, if the kicking of the
plaintiff by the defendant was an unlawful act, the intention of defendant to kick
him was also unlawful." 80 Wis. at 527, 50 N.W. 403. Indeed, the case is a good
illustration of the general proposition that the prima facie case is complete without
reference to negligence or intent. Here the "intent" requirement is not satisfied if
the specific intent to harm must be shown on the strength of the criminal law anal-
ogies, for the jury found expressly for the defendant on this point. The court in
effect eliminates the intent requirement by fiction, and allows the plaintiff full
recovery on the ground that the defendant kicked him.
[17]The doctrinal basis for the defense of contributory negligence in battery cases is
not clear under the modern law. There are statements that it should not be applied
in cases of intentional torts because "where the defendant's conduct is actually
intended to inflict harm upon the plaintiff, there is a difference, not merely in
degree but in the kind of fault; and the defense never has been extended to such intentional torts." William L. Prosser, *supra* chap. III, note 2, at 426. But this argument is flawed because it assumes that all cases of battery require proof of specific
intent to harm. However, in his earlier discussion of intentional torts Prosser notes

tween the two parties, the plaintiff is in a better position to take steps which will reduce the harm that will result from contact, and so should be required to take those steps.

If this line of reasoning is accepted, the defendant in cases like *Vosburg v. Putney* could argue that the plaintiff was in breach of his duties to the defendant when he failed, say, to wear a shin-guard which at low cost would protect him from accidental harm. The distinction between acts and omissions that appears to be immaterial in the formulation (though not the practice) of negligence law when applied to the defendant's conduct should be immaterial as well when it is plaintiff's conduct that is to be taken into account. But the law does not take this position. It holds instead that the plaintiff is under no duty to package and bandage himself (though the costs are low) in order to reduce the damages to be paid by those who might harm him. Where the plaintiff is in a weakened condition, he has not caused the harm in any of the senses developed in chapter III, even if he had the opportunity to prevent them from occurring. As in the case of the good Samaritan, one man is not under a common law duty to take steps to aid a stranger.[18]

The common law position on the good Samaritan question does not appeal to our highest sense of benevolence and charity, and it is not at all surprising that there have been many proposals for its alteration or abolition. Let us here examine but one of these proposals. After concluding that the then (1908) current position of the law led to intolerable results, James Barr Ames argued that the appropriate rule should be as follows:

> One who fails to interfere to save another from impending death or great bodily harm, when he might do so with little or no incon-

---

that the term does not cover only cases in which there is "a desire to do any harm. Rather it is an intent to bring about a result which will invade the interests of another in a way that the law will not sanction." *Id.* at 31. Since Vosburg does not involve specific intent to harm, it should be a case of battery in which the defense is admitted, even if the general rule is to the contrary.

[18]The application of this maxim is not limited to cases of personal injury. In the famous case of Leroy Fibre v. Chicago, Mil. & St. Paul R.R., 232 U.S. 340 (1914), the Supreme Court ruled that the defendant could not make out a good defense of contributory negligence by showing that the plaintiff stored flammable flax within 75 to 100 feet of the defendant's tracks even though it might have been cheaper for the plaintiff to move his flax than for the defendant to control the sparks emitted by the operation of its trains.

> venience to himself, and the death or great bodily harm follows as a consequence of his inaction, shall be punished criminally and shall make compensation to the party injured or to his widow and children in case of death.[19]

Even this solution, however, does not satisfy the *Carroll Towing* formula. The general use of the cost-benefit analysis required under the economic interpretation of negligence does not permit a person to act on the assumption that he may as of right attach special weight and importance to his own welfare. Under Ames's good Samaritan rule, a defendant in cases of affirmative acts would be required to take only those steps that can be done "with little or no inconvenience." But if the distinction between causing harm and not preventing harm is to be disregarded, why should the difference in standards between the two cases survive the reform of the law? The only explanation is that the two situations are regarded at bottom as raising totally different issues, even for those who insist upon the immateriality of this distinction. Even those who argue, as Ames does, that the law is utilitarian must in the end find some special place for the claims of egoism which are an inseparable byproduct of the belief that individual autonomy— individual liberty— is a good in itself not explainable in terms of its purported social worth. It is one thing to *allow* people to act as they please in the belief that the "invisible hand" will provide the happy congruence of the individual and the social good. Such a theory, however, at bottom must regard individual autonomy as but a means to some social end. It takes a great deal more to assert

---

[19] James Barr Ames, *supra* chap. II, note 3, at 113. See also Wallace M. Rudolph, The Duty to Act: A Proposed Rule, 44 Neb. L. Rev. 499 (1965), for a more complicated rule which states: "A person has a duty to act whenever (1) The harm or loss is imminent and there is apparently no other practical alternative to avoid the threatened harm or loss except his own action; (2) Failure to act would result in substantial harm or damage to another person or his property and the effort, risk, or cost of acting is disproportionately less than the harm or damage avoided; and (3) The circumstances placing the person in a position to act are purely fortuitous." *Id.* at 509.

The first and second conditions are open to the same sorts of objections as Ames's rule, but the third seeks to limit the scope of its application. Nonetheless, its effect does not appear to be too great, for Rudolph says: "Thus though condition three protects the classic rich from being obligated to the classic poor, it does allow, under limited circumstances, a person of means who is temporarily without funds to require someone else to lend him money, if the resources to be saved by lending the money exceed substantially the risk of losing the money." *Id.* at 510. See p. 63, *infra,* for a discussion of forced exchanges.

that men are *entitled* to act as they choose (within the limits of strict liability) even though it is certain that there will be cases where individual welfare will be in conflict with the social good.[20] Only then is it clear that even freedom has its costs—costs revealed in the acceptance of the good Samaritan doctrine.

But are the alternatives more attractive? Once one decides that as a matter of statutory or common law duty, an individual is required under some circumstances to act at his own cost for the exclusive benefit of another, then it is very hard to set out in a principled manner the limits of social interference with individual liberty. Suppose one claims, as Ames does, that his proposed rule applies only in the "obvious" cases where everyone (or almost everyone) would admit that the duty was appropriate: to the case of the man upon the bridge who refuses to throw a rope to a stranger drowning in the waters below. Even if the rule starts out with such modest ambitions, it is difficult to confine it to those limits. Take a simple case first. *X* as a representative of a private charity asks you for $10 in order to save the life of some starving child in a country ravaged by war. There are other donors available but the number of needy children exceeds that number. The money means "nothing" to you. Are you under a legal obligation to give the $10? Or to lend it interest-free? Does $10 amount to a substantial cost or inconvenience within the meaning of Ames's rule? It is true that the relationship between the gift to charity and the survival of an unidentified child is not so apparent as is the relationship between the man upon the bridge and the swimmer caught in the swirling seas. But lest the physical imagery govern, it is clear in both cases that someone will die as a consequence of your inaction in both cases. Is there a duty to give, or is the contribution a matter of charity?

Consider yet another example where services, not cash, are in issue. Ames insists that his rule would not require the only surgeon in India capable of saving the life of a person with a given affliction to travel across the subcontinent to perform an operation, presumably because the inconvenience and cost would be

---

[20]"Each person possesses an inviolability founded on justice that even the welfare of society as a whole cannot override. For this reason justice denies that the loss of freedom for some is made right by a greater good shared by others. It does not allow that the sacrifices imposed on a few are outweighed by the larger sum of advantages enjoyed by many." John Rawls, A Theory of Justice 3-4 (1971).

substantial.[21] But how would he treat the case if some third person were willing to pay him for all of his efforts? If the payment is sufficient to induce the surgeon to act, then there is no need for the good Samaritan doctrine at all. But if it is not, then it is again necessary to compare the costs of the physician with the benefits to his prospective patient. It is hard to know whether Ames would require the forced exchange under these circumstances. But it is at least arguable that under his theory forced exchanges should be required, since the payment might reduce the surgeon's net inconvenience to the point where it was trivial.

Once forced exchanges, regardless of the levels of payment, are accepted, it will no longer be possible to delineate the sphere of activities in which contracts (or charity) will be required in order to procure desired benefits and the sphere of activity in which those benefits can be procured as of right. Where tests of "reasonableness"—stated with such confidence, and applied with such difficulty—dominate the law of tort, it becomes impossible to tell where liberty ends and obligation begins; where contract ends, and tort begins. In each case, it will be possible for some judge or jury to decide that there was something else which the defendant should have done, and he will decide that on the strength of some cost-benefit formula that is difficult indeed to apply. These remarks are conclusive, I think, against the adoption of Ames's rule by judicial innovation, and they bear heavily on the desirability of the abandonment of the good Samaritan rule by legislation as well. It is not surprising that the law has, in the midst of all the clamor for reform, remained unmoved in the end, given the inability to form alternatives to the current position.[22]

But the defense of the common law rule on the good Samaritan does not rest solely upon a criticism of its alternatives. Strong

---

[21] For an extended discussion of the duties of a professional physician, see Wallace M. Rudolph, *supra* note 19, at 512–19, whose proposed rule indeed requires a high standard of conduct.

[22] "Such decisions are revolting to any moral sense. They have been denounced with vigor by legal writers. Thus far the difficulties of setting any standards of unselfish service to fellow men, and of making any workable rule to cover possible situations where fifty people might fail to rescue one, has limited any tendency to depart from the rule to cases where some special relation between the parties has afforded a justification for the creation of a duty, without any question of setting up a rule of universal application." William L. Prosser, *supra* chap. III, note 2, at 341 (3d ed.).

arguments can be advanced to show that the common law position on the good Samaritan problem is in the end consistent with both moral and economic principles.

The history of Western ethics has been marked by the development of two lines of belief. One line of moral thought emphasizes the importance of freedom of the will. It is the intention (or motive) that determines the worth of the act; and no act can be moral unless it is performed free from external compulsion.[23] Hence the expansion of the scope of positive law could only reduce the moral worth of human action. Even if positive law could ensure conformity to the appropriate external standards of conduct, it, like other forms of external constraints, destroys the moral worth of the act. Hence the elimination of the positive law becomes a minimum condition for moral conduct, even if it means that persons entitled to benefits (in accordance with some theory of entitlements respected but not enforced) will not receive them if their fellow men are immoral.

On the other hand there are those theories that concern themselves not with the freedom of the will, but with the external effects of individual behavior. There is no room for error, because each act which does not further the stated goals (usually the maximization of welfare) is in terms of these theories a bad act. Thus a system of laws must either require the individual to act, regardless of motive, in the socially desired manner, or create incentives for him to so behave. Acceptance of this kind of theory has as its corollary the acceptance, if necessary, of an elaborate system of legal rules to ensure compliance with the stated goals of maximization even if individual liberty (which now only counts as a kind of satisfaction) is sacrificed in the effort.

At a common sense level, neither of these views is accepted in its pure form. The strength of each theory lays bare the weaknesses of the other. Preoccupation with the moral freedom of a given actor ignores the effects of his conduct upon other persons. Undue emphasis upon the conformity to external standards of behavior entails a loss of liberty. Hence, most systems of conventional morality try to distinguish between those circumstances in which a person should be compelled to act for the benefit of his fellow man, and those cases where he should be allowed to do so only if prompted by the appropriate motives. To put the point in other terms, the distinction is taken between that conduct which is required and that which, so to speak, is beyond the call of duty. If that distinction is accepted as part of a common morality, then the argument in favor of the good Samaritan rule is that it, better than any possible alternatives, serves to mark off the first class of activities from the second. Compensation for harm caused can be demanded in accordance with the principles of strict liability. Failure to aid those in need can invoke at most moral censure on the ground that the person so accused did not voluntarily conform his conduct to some "universal" principle of justice. The rules of causation, which create liability in the first case, deny it in the second. It may well be that the conduct of individuals who do not aid fellow men is under some circumstances outrageous, but it does not follow that a legal system that does not enforce a duty to aid is outrageous as well.

The defense of the good Samaritan rule in economic terms takes the same qualified form. The cost-benefit analysis has in recent literature been regarded as the best means for the solution of all problems of social organization in those cases where market transactions are infeasible. On that view, the basic principles of economics become a most powerful instrument for the achievement of social justice. But there is another strand of economic thought—more skeptical in its conclusions—which emphasizes the limitations of economic theory for the solution of legal problems.

Most economics textbooks accept that the premises of economic theory do not permit so-called interpersonal comparisons of utility. Thus Kenneth Arrow states: "The viewpoint will be taken here that interpersonal comparison of utilities has no meaning and, in fact, that there is no meaning relevant to welfare comparisons in the measurability of individual utility."[24] In effect, all attempts to compare costs and benefits between different persons require in the end some noneconomic assumption to measure trade-offs in utility between them. Where no noneconomic assumptions are made, it follows that, in strict theory, an economist can make utility comparisons between alternative social arrangements only under a very restricted set of conditions. One social arrangement can be pronounced superior to a second alternative only if (1) it can be shown that everybody is at least as

[23]See, e.g., James Street Fulton, The Free Person and Legal Authority, in Responsibility in Law and in Morals 1–11 (Arthur L. Harding ed. 1960).

[24]Kenneth Arrow, Social Choice and Individual Values 9 (2d ed. 1963).

well off under the first alternative as he is under the second, and (2) at least one person is better off under the first system than he is under the second. If these conditions are respected, then no strictly economic judgment can be made between alternative social states where one person under the allegedly preferred state is worse off than he is under the next best alternative. Yet it is precisely that kind of situation that is involved whenever there is a legal dispute. In economic terms, the resolution of every dispute requires a trade-off between the parties, for no one has yet found a way in which both parties could win a lawsuit. In order to decide the case of the good Samaritan, therefore, we must make the very kind of interpersonal comparisons of utility which economic theory cannot make in its own terms.

There is one possible escape from this problem. It could be argued that the defendant should be held liable because if the parties had the opportunity to contract between themselves, they doubtless would have agreed that the defendant should assume the obligation to save the plaintiff in his time of distress. Thus one could argue that (in the absence of externalities) an agreement between two persons can only have favorable welfare effects since each person will be better off on account of the voluntary exchange. On this view the function of the law of tort is to anticipate those contractual arrangements which parties would have made had the transactions costs been low enough to permit direct negotiations.

This position, however, is subject to objections. The courts have struggled for years to determine the content of incomplete and ambiguous contracts which were actually negotiated by the parties. There at least they could look to, among other things, the language of the relevant documents, the custom of the trade, and the history of the prior negotiations. In the good Samaritan context, there are no documents, no customs, and no prior negotiations. The courts have only the observation that the parties would have contracted to advance their mutual interests. Given the infinite variation in terms (what price? what services?) that we could expect to find in such contracts, it is difficult to believe that that theoretical observation could enable us to determine or even approximate any bargain which the parties might have made if circumstances had permitted. It is for good reason that the courts have always refused to make contracts for the parties.

But there is a further point. We are concerned with the enforcement of a contract by private action when one of the parties objects to its performance. It no longer seems possible to argue that both parties are better off on account of the contract since one party has indicated his desire to repudiate it. Even though the theory of the underlying action is shifted from tort to some extended form of contract, the difficulties raised by the rule that forbids interpersonal comparison of utilities still remain. At the time of the enforcement, one party argues not for an *exchange* which makes both parties better off, but for a *transfer* of wealth which makes him better off. Again we must find some way—some theory of fairness—which can explain which of them is to be made better off. Welfare economics cannot provide the answer because it cannot accommodate the trade-offs which are part and parcel of legal decisions.

Even after these arguments are made, many people will be concerned with the social costs of a system of rules which does not purport to have an economic base. But in a social sense it should be clear that people will act in a manner to minimize their losses, regardless of the legal rules adopted. Once people know that others are not obliged to assist them in their time of peril, they will on their own take steps to keep from being placed in a position where they will need assistance where none may be had. These precautions may not eliminate losses in the individual case, but they should reduce the number of cases in which such losses should occur.

In addition, the incentive effects created by the absence of a good Samaritan rule must be examined in the context of other rules of substantive law. Thus it is critical to ask about the incentives created by rules that permit a rescuer to bring an action against the person he saved on quasi-contractual theories. It is also important to ask what modifications of behavior could be expected if the scope of this kind of action were expanded, and important, too, to know about the possible effects of systems of public honors and awards for good Samaritans. None of these arguments is designed to show that the common law approach can be justified on economic grounds, but they do show how perilous it is to attempt to justify legal rules by the incentives that they create.

The same kinds of observations apply to the maxim that a tortfeasor must take his victim as he finds him. It is true that the rule reduces the plaintiff's incentives to take care of himself even where he is able to do so efficiently. But it is a mistake to think that any legal rule on this question can create strong incentives. Indeed, it seems far more likely that few plaintiffs will be prepared to take unnecessary risks of personal injury even if they know that they will be able to recover in full for the injuries from a defendant who caused them. Damages in tort still do not permit a plaintiff to make a profit; and in some cases it is arguable that they do not permit recovery of adequate compensation. Some men may be moved to guide their conduct by general statements of substantive law, but in most cases any incentives created by the selection of one legal rule in preference to another will be masked by the fear of injury which is shared by defendants and plaintiffs alike.

But it is a mistake to dwell too long upon questions of cost, for they should not be decisive in the analysis of the individual cases. Instead it is better to see the law of torts in terms of what might be called its political function. The arguments made here suggest that the first task of the law of torts is to define the boundaries of individual liberty. To this question the rules of strict liability, based upon the twin notions of causation and volition, provide a better answer than the alternative theories based upon the notion of negligence, whether explicated in moral or economic terms. In effect, the principles of strict liability say that the liberty of one person ends when he causes harm to another. Until that point he is free to act as he chooses, and need not take into account the welfare of others.

But the law of tort does not end with the recognition of individual liberty. Once a man causes harm to another, he has brought himself within the boundaries of the law of tort. It does not follow, however, that he will be held liable in each and every case in which it can be showed that he caused harm, for it may still be possible for him to escape liability, not by an insistence upon his freedom of action, but upon a specific showing that his conduct was either excused or justified. Thus far we have only made occasional and unsystematic references to the problems raised by both pleas of excuses and justification. Their systematic explication remains crucial to the further development of the law of tort. That task, however, is large enough to deserve special attention of its own.

PART TWO

Defenses and Subsequent Pleas
in a
Theory of Strict Liability

V. Introduction

In this essay, I hope to press forward with the task begun in Part One: to show how the tort law can be viewed usefully as a system of corrective justice appropriate for the redress of private harms. This aim is neither new nor novel; it is the implicit assumption upon which the common law approach to the law of torts has rested throughout most of its long history. There is, however, one additional assumption in this history which I believe to be as erroneous as it is deep-seated, and to which both this and the preceding essay are directed. It has been taken as a settled premise that the tort law must assume the contours of the modern law of negligence if the primary preoccupation of tort law is justice in the particular case. The system of strict liability, which is the major alternative to the law of negligence, has been dismissed almost out of hand as a primitive and amoral system of liability, and the pockets of strict liability that have been retained in the modern law have been regarded as vestiges that have no place in modern systems of jurisprudence.[1]

A most unsatisfactory feature of the traditional debates between the theories of negligence and the theories of strict liability is that while the law of negligence has been worked out in great detail, the system of strict liability has not; instead it has been generally treated as though it involved little more than the simple

NOTE: I am much indebted to Walter Blum, Harry Kalven, Jr., Hein D. Kötz, and John H. Langbein for their valuable comments on an earlier draft of these chapters. I should also like to thank the American Bar Foundation for its assistance and support during the research for and preparation of this essay. The views expressed here are, of course, my own and not those of the Foundation.—RAE

[1]See, *e.g.,* James Barr Ames, Law and Morals, 22 Harv. L. Rev. 97 (1908).

proposition, whoever harms pays.[2] This notion, be it primitive or not, has an irreducible role to play in the formation of a just system of tort law. Yet it represents not the full development of the system, but only its initial premise. Needed beyond this original premise is a detailed account of the set of limitations that must be added to it. Only then can we pass judgment upon the comparative worth of a system of strict liability with a knowledge of what that system entails.

This essay, then, tries to develop an alternative to the law of negligence within the tradition that views the tort law as a system of corrective justice. As such the article stands in opposition to a more recent trend in the law that tries to explain and justify the rules of tort law solely as means to achieve an efficient use of resources. The economic approach has been used in recent years to support and refine both systems of negligence[3] and systems of strict liability.[4] In defense of torts as a system of corrective justice, I hope, first, to show that it is not possible to make the central choices between these two systems by reference to economic criteria, and, second, to identify within the framework of a system of strict liability those particular sorts of issues to which economic arguments might be relevant.

This inquiry into the principles of tort law cannot, I believe, be sensibly pursued by a search for a formal definition of the term "justice." Such a definition, even if found, could do little to decide concrete cases. As an alternative approach, I think that the best way to shape the inquiry is to resort to a traditional technique of the law—the development of an elaborate network of substantive presumptions which will allow us to reach sound systematic results by an indefinite series of approximations, each of which will move us closer to a fuller statement of the substantive law.[5]

---

[2] "It is widely agreed that strict liability does not mean absolutely unlimited liability. In the present state of the law there is considerable difficulty in tracing the exact limitations." Charles O. Gregory & Harry Kalven, Jr., Cases and Materials on Torts, 579 (2d ed. 1969). Gregory and Kalven devote about five pages to these limitations, but many times that amount to the limitations upon liability in the negligence system.

[3] See, *e.g.,* Richard A. Posner, A Theory of Negligence, 1 J. Leg. Studies 29 (1972).

[4] See, *e.g.,* Guido Calabresi & Jon T. Hirschoff, Toward a Test for Strict Liability in Torts, 81 Yale L.J. 1055 (1972).

[5] For a more detailed account of what a system of presumptions entails, see Richard A. Epstein, Pleadings and Presumptions, 40 U. Chi. L. Rev. 556 (1973).

These presumptions do not necessarily decide a case in a given manner, but each indicates that the result must go one way on the strength of the facts alleged unless the other party to the case is able to give some "good reason" why it should not.

This scheme of presumptions receives extended use in the law, for all procedural systems divide the elements of a case into those appropriate to its claim and defense. That simple division, however, is incomplete in one crucial respect, for it ignores the possibility that a valid defense may still be subject to exceptions of its own: If a valid prima facie case only creates the presumption that the defendant should be held responsible, so too a valid defense should create only the presumption that he should not. Therefore it should be proper in principle, and appropriate in many factual situations, for the plaintiff to reply to a valid defense with some new substantive allegation consistent with the previous pleas that will once again reestablish the balance of equities in his favor. In principle that allegation in turn is subject to exceptions of its own, and so on, until issue is ultimately joined on a question of fact or law. The major strength of this scheme is that it not only allows us to identify those elements essential to the development of a theory, but it also enables us to specify the sequence in which they become material. Allegations in a reply, for example, can never be collapsed into the plaintiff's prima facie case, because they are material to decision not in all cases of a given type, but only after the defendant has interposed a valid affirmative defense.[6] The method here therefore differs from that implicitly adopted in the law of negligence. The negligence law tries in its analysis of "reasonableness" to fit as many of the factors that bear on responsibility into the statement of the prima facie case as possible. The approach here is to say only as little as is necessary at any given time to shift the balance between the parties.[7]

The kind of formal system adopted here does not of itself permit the decision of particular cases in the absence of a commitment to some substantive principles. The first of these principles, and one accepted by all legal systems, is that the plaintiff must

---

[6]*Id.* at 566–71.

[7]Even here there is one major qualification, for I reserve the treatment of deliberate harms for a later paper.

first show some reason why the defendant should be obligated to him. The second point is related to the first. As only the plaintiff and the defendant are parties to the suit at hand, only the equities between them should be taken into account in its resolution. These equities, moreover, must, I believe, be designed to show not that it is unfortunate that one party will be burdened with a loss, lest every accident however caused be the source of a lawsuit. Instead they must satisfy a stronger condition and show why it is that the loss is better placed upon one party than another.[8]

Given these premises, I argued in the first essay on torts that the plaintiff stated a prima facie case whenever he could show that the defendant had caused physical harm to his person or property, regardless of whether he intended to harm the plaintiff or had conducted his activities with reasonable care. This causal allegation shows that the condition of the plaintiff is linked as a matter of fact to the conduct of the defendant even before the imposition of tortious liability, and thereby permits the plaintiff to show that the initial balance between the two parties is in need of redress because of the defendant's conduct. The defendant has hurt the plaintiff, and not the other way around.

The simple assertion of the importance of causal notions in tort law is not the same, however, as an analysis of what they entail. In an attempt to dispel some of the confusion that surrounds the use of causal notions, I then isolated the four most common causal paradigms used in both ordinary speech and legal analysis.[9] The first of these rests on the simple notion of the use of force and is

[8]Thus this principle requires that the plaintiff cannot recover from the defendant simply because he was injured, or was injured by some third party. In the first case the plaintiff has no action at all, and in the second he must pursue his remedy against the party that caused the harm. Indeed, it follows from the general principle that the conduct of a third party is never a reason to decide the instant case in one manner or the other. The appropriate response is first to adjust the equities between the parties to the intitial suit, and then to allow the loser to pursue his cause of action, if any, against the third party. For application of this principle, see *supra* chap. III, pp. 32–35.

[9]See *supra* chap. III, pp. 23–49. It is possible to generate still others, as with the tort of false imprisonment, where the prima facie case should be "*A* imprisoned *B*." The false, *i.e.* wrong, element of the case is explicated not by reference to negligence or intent, but by the possible exceptions to the prima facie case. This paradigm, like all the others, preserves the causal dominance of *A*'s act in relation to *B*'s injury.

captured in the proposition, *A* hit *B*, with its simple transitive structure. The second paradigm, *A* frightened *B*, has much the same grammatical structure as the first, but requires us to take into account *B*'s response to *A*'s actions in order to complete the causal chain. The third paradigm, *A* made *B* hit *C*, states a connection between *A* and *C* only through the acts of *B* which *A* compelled, and thus requires us to take into account the behavior of a third party. The last of these paradigms, *A* created a dangerous condition that resulted in *B*'s harm, demands a detailed analysis of, first, the kinds of conditions that should be regarded as dangerous, and, second, the impact of the actions or events that intervened between *A*'s conduct and *B*'s harm. For all of their internal differences, each of these paradigms reveals a domination of *A*, the author of the action, over *B*, its object, that prima facie calls for redress by the law of torts. In order to show, moreover, how causal relations could prove indispensable to recovery under some circumstances, I discussed at length the problem of the good Samaritan as an instance of a case where the plaintiff must fail for want of a causal connection between his own harm and the defendant's conduct.

In this paper I propose to continue the development of a system of tort law in which the allegation that "the defendant caused plaintiff harm" states a good prima facie case. In order to develop that system, I shall consider first the class of defenses that I believe should be treated as ineffective as a matter of principle. Some of these pleas are of small practical importance, but all of them have great theoretical significance for the development of the system. Next I shall discuss three different kinds of defenses— causal defenses, the defense of assumption of risk, and the defense of plaintiff's trespass, together with their replies and subsequent pleas—that I believe should be incorporated into a general system of tort liability. Their inclusion in the procedural framework outlined above reflects formal as well as substantive concerns. The results will at times sound unfamiliar, though I hope neither artificial nor contrived. By this analysis, which pays attention to both formal and substantive questions, I hope to show that it is possible to incorporate into a single conceptual framework the disparate notions whose place in tort law seems unquestioned to common understanding but whose exact role remains uncertain.

VI. Ineffective Defenses

The first two insufficient defenses can be conveniently considered as a pair. These are the defenses of, first, private necessity,[1] and, second, compulsion imposed upon the defendant by the acts or threats of a third party. The argument against the recognition of both these defenses is that they are attempts by the defendant to shift the costs of his own problems onto the shoulders of the plaintiff. Consider the situation where the defendant, when faced with these same external threats—a severe storm or an attack by a third party—responds in a manner that harms himself or his own property. In these circumstances it is clear that he could not under any legal theory find a way to hold a stranger, one who did not create the danger, accountable for all or part of the loss that he has suffered. Essentially the same problem arises when that defendant in the course of his efforts to escape from that same external compulsion inflicts, in any of the causal senses developed, harm upon the plaintiff. The only proper question for tort law is whether the plaintiff or the defendant will be required to bear the loss. The argument here is only that it is fairer to require the defendant to bear the loss because he had the hard choice of harming or being harmed when, given what is alleged, the plaintiff had no choice at all. The plaintiff's causal plea creates a nexus between the parties; the defendant's answer does not. Prima facie, one man should not be allowed to solve his own problems at the expense of physical harm to another. The rejection of these two defenses assures that a man who injures another will be treated, to the extent possible, as though he had injured himself.

These arguments apply with equal force to the twin pleas of infancy and insanity. The only difference is that the defendant's

---

[1]The defendant enters a plea of private necessity when he argues that natural forces compelled him to harm the plaintiff's interests in order to protect his own. See generally William L. Prosser, Handbook of the Law of Torts, § 24 (4th ed. 1971).

problems stem, not from the threat of forces from without, but from the defects of his own personal condition. The question, as before, is not whether it is fair for an insane person to be held responsible for the harm he has caused, but only whether it is fairer for him or for the plaintiff to bear those costs. Once it is accepted that the plaintiff is not to be held accountable for (say) the defendant's insanity, in the sense that he is in no way obliged to look after him and provide for his general support, it follows that he should not be required to assume in effect the burdens of guardianship to the extent that the defendant has harmed him.[2] Only if the defendant is denied the benefit of the plea of insanity will he, and not some stranger cast as plaintiff, be required to bear those costs and to treat the harm he has inflicted upon others as though it were inflicted upon himself. Again the causal plea develops a nexus between the parties that the plea of insanity does not. The argument proceeds along parallel lines if the plea of infancy is substituted for that of insanity.

The rejection of both these pleas is thus straightforward, given that we are working within a theory of strict liability.[3] Their proper role in the context of the law of negligence is more difficult to determine. The present law of negligence treats infancy and insanity not as independent defenses, but as elements to be taken into account in passing on the reasonableness of the defendant's conduct. Yet no reason is provided why these defects should be taken into account in any way to decide whether or not defendant

[2]The argument in the text is essentially that of Thomas M. Cooley, A Treatise on the Law of Torts or the Wrongs which Arise Independent of Contract, 100–02 (1879): "[There is] no more propriety or justice in making others bear the losses resulting from his unreasoning fury when it is spent upon them or their property, than there would be in calling upon them to pay the expense of his confinement in an asylum when his own estate is ample for the purpose." Cooley also suggests that insanity should not excuse conduct prima facie tortious in order to create an incentive for his personal guardian or the beneficiary of his estate to take the appropriate steps to keep the insane person out of trouble. *Id.* at 100. If it is desired to create these incentives, it should be done by imposing direct liability upon the parties to be charged. Francis H. Bohlen, Liability in Torts of Infants and Insane Persons, 23 Mich. L. Rev. 9, 34 n.38 (1924), reprinted in his Studies on the Law of Torts 543, 574 n.39 (1926); George J. Alexander & Thomas S. Szasz, Mental Illness as an Excuse for Civil Wrongs, 43 Notre Dame Lawyer 24, 35–36 (1967).

[3]"Wherever a liability is imposed irrespective of fault there is no reason why an infant or insane person should not be as fully liable as a normal person." Francis H. Bohlen, 23 Mich. L. Rev., *supra* note 2, at 33, reprinted in his Studies, *supra* note 2, at 572–73. The modern cases, moreover, support this result, even though judges are aware that the results cannot easily be fitted into a system of negligence. See, *e.g.,* McGuire v. Almy, 297 Mass. 323, 8 N.E.2d 760 (1937).

complies with the general standard imposed by law, given that other defects of mind and body are regarded as part of that "personal equation" which it is not the law's business to notice.[4] If the slips of a man "born hasty and awkward" are troublesome to his neighbors,[5] then so too are those of the infant or insane person.[6]

The uneasy accommodation of infancy within the law of negligence is further revealed by an important exception to the general rule that an infant is to be judged by a standard of care appropriate to his personal condition. Thus it is generally held that an infant's conduct will be measured by the standards applicable to an adult in those cases in which he engages in adultlike activities. The ground is that if he wants the benefits of behaving like an adult, he must bear the costs of being an adult.[7] The most important application of this rule occurs in the case of automobile drivers, which means that in the great bulk of tort cases the exception and not the general rule is applied. Nonetheless, the distinction creates impossible problems of application, particularly since it is not clear what test should be used in order to decide when the infant acts like an infant and when he acts like an adult. Playing ball, using mechanical equipment, riding bicycles, and the like, are all sorts of things that are done in the normal course of events by both infants and adults.[8] It takes but little ingenuity to allow

[4]For an exhaustive account of the treatment of different individual attributes under the negligence law, see Warren A. Seavey, Negligence—Subjective or Objective?, 41 Harv. L. Rev. 1 (1927).

[5]Holmes notes that infancy and insanity are exceptions to the general rule that the personal equation is not taken into account in passing on the reasonableness of defendant's conduct, but does not explain why these particular defects should be treated differently from others the defendant may have. Oliver Wendell Holmes, Jr., The Common Law 108–09 (1881). He does argue that it is unfair to hold an infant or insane person to a standard of care impossible for him to achieve, but the same reason appears to apply with equal force to persons whose congenital defects make it impossible for them to conform to the appropriate standard of care.

[6]Nor can the problem be concealed by an appeal to formulas that ask the jury to determine "What it is reasonable to expect of children of like age, intelligence, and experience." William L. Prosser, *supra* note 1, at 155. The same question could be asked of idiots, but it is not. The point is that the law of negligence cannot decide whether to base its rules upon the equities between the parties or upon the personal blame of the defendant alone.

[7]*Id.* at 156–57; Restatement of Torts 2d, § 283A, comment b. "[I]t would be unfair to the public to permit a minor in the operation of a motor vehicle to observe any other standards of care and conduct than those expected of all others." Dellwo v. Pearson, 259 Minn. 452, 458, 107 N.W.2d 859, 863 (1961).

[8]The point is not, however, always accepted. "We agree that minors are entitled to be judged by standards commensurate with their age, experience, and wisdom

79

the exception to swallow the rule. True the distinction between the two classes of activities has been defended on the ground that "[a] person observing an infant at play . . . may anticipate conduct that does not reach an adult standard of care or prudence."[9] But the rationale is not congruent with the exception, for not all persons are injured while observing infants at play, and for those who are, the point should be material not on the defense of infancy but on that of assumption of risk.[10]

The catalogue of insufficient defenses should include the defendant's appeals to his virtue as well as those to his problems and weaknesses. Thus, he should not be permitted to plead as an affirmative defense that he used his best efforts to avoid harming the plaintiff, or, to rephrase the point, that the defendant did all in his power to see that his actions did not harm the plaintiff.[11] These pleas bear a close resemblance to the allegation of negligence required of the plaintiff under the modern systems, but are not identical to it. The negligence plea in its complete form makes reference both to notions of duty and to causation. It allows the defendant to prevail even where he is in breach of his duty of care, if he can show that his breach of duty bears no causal relation to the plaintiff's harm. The plea of "best efforts," however formulated, does not admit of this possibility, but unconditionally

---

when engaged in activities appropriate to their age, experience, and wisdom. Hence, when children are walking, running, playing with toys, throwing balls, operating bicycles, sliding or engaged in other childhood activities their conduct should be judged by the rule of what is reasonable conduct under the circumstances among which are the age, experience, and stage of mental development of the minor involved." Daniels v. Evans, 107 N.H. 407-08, 224 A.2d 63-64 (1966). Not surprisingly, the exception that holds infants to adult standards has had a checkered history. It has been applied to motorcycles, as in Daniels v. Evans, but not to bicycles. Williams v. Gilbert, 239 Ark. 935, 395 S.W.2d 333 (1965). It has also been applied to teenage golfers. Neumann v. Shlansky, 312 N.Y.S.2d 951 (1970). The golf case is important as a theoretical matter because it shows that the rule that treats infants like adults does not apply only to activities that are licensed for the protection of the public.

[9]Dellwo v. Pearson, 259 Minn. 452, 458, 107 N.W. 2d 859, 863 (1961). The court there held that power boats are within the exception.

[10]See *infra* pp. 97-116.

[11]The plea in answer to the prima facie case is put in these words by Choke, C.J.: "but he should have said that he could not do it in any other manner or that he did all that was in his power to keep them [*i.e.,* the cut thorns] out." The Thorns Case, Y.B., Mich. 6 Ed. IV, f.7, pl. 18 (1466). The case is important because Judge Littleton does not accept the defense but opts instead for strict liability, and thereby sets up the tension in the tort law that persists to the present day.

requires the defendant to use all the care within his power to avoid the harm in question.[12] Again, the plea specifies a uniquely subjective standard against which to judge the defendant's conduct, and thus does not allow for that peculiar compromise between objective and subjective notions that characterizes the analysis of reasonableness under the negligence theory. One ground on which to reject this plea is a narrow one: How could the defendant ever claim to use best efforts when by hypothesis he did not choose to do nothing at all? But if it is then said that this extreme position is not what is meant by the plea, its thrust can be only that the risks to the plaintiff created by the defendant's activities were as small as his best efforts could make them, where it is taken as a given that the defendant has the right to carry out these "lawful" activities for his own exclusive benefit. At that point the plea raises only those issues presented by the economic view of negligence captured in the *Carroll Towing* formula. If it is accepted that the assignment of the risk for a certain activity should not be a function of its magnitude, then this plea must fail as reconstrued, for it is only another attempt to reintroduce the doctrines of negligence together with their economic overtones into the law of tort.[13]

The last of the ineffective defenses that I propose to consider is applicable only to land and goods, and it asserts that the defendant took or destroyed the plaintiff's property in the mistaken belief that it was his own.[14] The question whether the property was used for the benefit of the defendant might be of some importance under a theory of restitution where the benefit to the defendant is less than the loss to the plaintiff. But a theory of strict liability in tort will allow the plaintiff to recover the full measure of his loss even if the law of restitution will not.[15] To restrict the plaintiff to the lower measure of recovery is to allow the defendant in effect to take the plaintiff's property at a price at

[12]See Richard A. Epstein, *supra* chap. V, note 5, at 574.

[13]For the discussion of that formula, see *supra* chap. II.

[14]The arguments apply with equal force to cases when the plaintiff mistakenly believed that he had the owner's permission to use or consume the property in question, so only the case of ownership will be considered in the text.

[15]The plaintiff may well be better off in restitution if the value to the defendant is greater than the loss he has suffered. If so, he should be allowed to switch his theory, for there is nothing about the theory of strict liability which says that it alone must provide the remedy on any given set of facts.

which he could not have purchased it. The plaintiff's prima facie case uses causal grounds to establish the link between his loss and the defendant's conduct. The defendant cannot establish any such linkage between the parties when he relies in defense upon his own mistake, be it reasonable or not. Thus the defense must be rejected on the same grounds as those that have already been considered.

The same result is reached under the modern systems of liability, all of which reject the plea of mistake as to ownership, whether that mistake be reasonable or not. It is difficult to reconcile that result with the general theory of negligence. The basic premise of the negligence system, whether based upon economic or moral conceptions of fault, is that the plaintiff must bear the costs of the reasonable risks taken by the defendant. There is no obvious reason why those risks assigned to the plaintiff do not include the defendant's reasonable mistakes as to the ownership of property.[16]

Each of the defenses considered and rejected in this section illustrates precisely the same problem: Do we look to the comparative equities between the parties or only to the personal condition of the defendant? The treatment that these defenses receive in the law of negligence reflects the tension in a theory which cannot select its basic premise. The theory of strict liability, however, does not seek to respect the second premise of the modern systems—that the defendant's conduct be measured against some external standard of social acceptability—and therefore is alone able to treat all these pleas in a consistent manner, a manner which demands that they not be accepted as affirmative defenses to the prima facie case.

---

[16]The result has also been defended on the ground that the defendant who appropriates the plaintiff's property in the mistaken belief that it is his own should be held responsible for the commission of an intentional tort. See Oliver Wendell Holmes, Jr., *supra* note 5, at 97. The prima facie case for the intentional tort, however, requires at a minimum not only that the defendant intend to deal with the property in question, but that he intends to deal with, and most likely to damage, the property of another. That difficulty cannot be gotten round, as Holmes suggests, by saying that the defendant "does intend to do the damage complained of," *id.* at 97, for the relational element of harm to another still must be established. Holmes is quite right to say that "[i]t would be odd if [the defendant] were to get rid of the burden by discovering that it belonged to his neighbor," *id.* at 97, but that is not an argument from intent; it is an elegant restatement of the principle of strict liability.

VII. Causal Defenses

The next group of defenses, unlike that just considered, does not concern the personal condition of the defendant, but deals instead with the plaintiff's conduct and the relationship it bears to the loss he has suffered. These defenses can be divided into two classes, one of which rests upon a further elaboration of causal notions, and the second of which does not.

In the preceding essay, I sought to isolate four common senses in which it is appropriate to say that a person's actions have caused physical harm.[1] Two points should be noted about these causal paradigms. First, it is possible, but by no means necessary, for more than one of them to apply to a given case, a point well taken at common law, which did not require that the defendant's conduct be the sole cause of the plaintiff's harm.[2] Second, these causal relations apply not only to the case where the defendant caused injury to the plaintiff, but also to the case where the plaintiff caused harm to himself, where, for example, the plaintiff hurt himself by driving his car into a lamp post.

The first class of effective defenses is designed, therefore, to take into account the causal arguments raised by defendant to excuse his own conduct. Consider the case where the plaintiff asserts as his prima facie case that he has been struck and injured by the defendant. In response to this prima facie case, the defendant could avoid the inference from causation to responsibility by appealing, for example, to the causal paradigm based upon fright

---

[1]See *supra* chap. III, pp. 23–49.

[2]The result is the same with a negligence standard: "In the typical case of contributory negligence both plaintiff and defendant would be liable to any third person injured by the accident." Fowler V. Harper & Fleming James, Jr., The Law of Torts 1199–1200 (1956). See also William L. Prosser, *supra* chap. VI, note 1, at 417.

or external compulsion, provided he could show that it was the plaintiff's conduct that induced or compelled the blow.

The argument in support of that defense runs as follows. Where the defendant could show only that he was made to harm the plaintiff by the conduct of a third person, he did not have a good defense to the plaintiff's prima facie case, but had instead a separate cause of action against the person who made him cause the harm.[3] That action is allowed on the strength of the judgment that as between the person who strikes the blow and the one who makes him do it, responsibility should rest with the latter. There is no reason to disturb that judgment as to causal priorities now that it is the plaintiff who induces, but does not deliver, the blow. Therefore the causal allegation raised by the defendant concerning the plaintiff's conduct should function as an effective defense within the framework of strict liability. There is no reason to require two actions, one by plaintiff against defendant, then another by defendant against plaintiff, to achieve the same result. Force has a causal priority only to the extent that it, unlike compulsion, must be present as a matter of fact in each case in which there is the infliction of physical harm. Yet compulsion, whether by force or fright, has a distinct priority over force in the sense that it determines responsibility where both are involved in the case, regardless of who is injured. "*A* hit *B*" states a good cause of action on *B*'s behalf to which "*B* compelled *A* to hit *B*" is a good defense. "*A* compelled *B* to hit himself" states a cause of action for which no causal defense is available to *A*.

Several observations should be made about these causal defenses. Notions of negligence and the closely associated notions of duty and "but for" causation have no more place here than in the statement of the prima facie case.[4] Again the defense is effective even if the defendant is unable to prove that the plaintiff acted unreasonably in compelling the defendant's blow, regardless of whether reasonableness receives its economic or moral interpretation.[5] The defense, moreover, raises no problems about

---

[3]See *supra* chap. III, pp. 32–33.

[4]For a criticism of "but for" causation, see *supra* chap. III, pp. 15–22, 44–45.

[5]For a discussion of the standard of conduct that the plaintiff can expect of the defendant when the plaintiff compelled defendant to hurt him, see *infra* chap. VIII at notes 33–34.

efficient use of resources because the plaintiff will take precisely the same steps whether he is held to a strict standard of conduct (though not of liability) or only to a negligence standard, for under both he can be expected to take precautions only if their expected benefits exceed their cost. As was the case with defendant's conduct, costs of legal administration apart, only the question of compensation turns on the choice of rule.[6]

Causal pleas can be used as defenses not only in cases of fright and compulsion but also in those of dangerous conditions that result in harm. The first of these paradigms was that of inherently dangerous conditions, of which the case of stored explosives is perhaps the best example. The second concerns objects dangerous on account of their position—like a rock perched at the edge of a cliff—whose potential energy can be released by the application of relatively small external force. The third dealt with the case of defective products whose use could result in harm. In each of these cases, the paradigms of dangerous conditions can be raised as defenses where the plaintiff created the dangerous condition in question even though the defendant's act was the immediate cause of plaintiff's harm. The priority between the competing causal paradigms of force and dangerous conditions is settled once it is agreed that a defendant whose use of force was the immediate cause of the harm has a prima facie case against a third party who created the dangerous condition upon which the force acted. The argument at this point is precisely what it was with the causal paradigms of compulsion, as again the use of causation as a defense forestalls the need for two actions that cancel out each other. The effect of the defense is to require that a man who carries explosives be held on causal grounds to bear the costs of his own harm if the explosives are set off by someone who hits him,[7]

---

[6]With the prima facie case, the reduction in the administrative costs for each case may be offset by the increased number of cases. It is possible (but unlikely) that there is no net reduction in administrative costs. See Richard A. Posner, Strict Liability: A Comment, 2 J. Leg. Studies 205, 209 (1973). Yet the administrative costs should be lower for the system where strict defenses are used in place of negligence defenses, as the strict plea reduces both the number of cases for decision and the cost of their resolution.

[7]Palsgraf v. Long Island R.R., 248 N.Y. 339, 162 N.E. 99 (1928), raises in a neat fashion the relationship between these two causal paradigms. There the defendant's conductor set off an explosive, held by a third person, that injured the plaintiff who was standing "many feet" away. If the person who carried the explosive had

that a man who knocks down and breaks an object left by its owner upon a precarious perch should be able to defend himself on causal grounds against the loss,[8] and that a man who uses a defective tool should prevail against the person who constructed it.[9]

The last paradigm of dangerous conditions concerns the case of the dangerous condition created when one person blocks or otherwise obstructs or interferes with the right of way of another and is of great importance for automobile and traffic accidents. The same arguments for causal priority apply here, so that if B blocks A's right of way, then prima facie A is entitled to prevail in any suit between them regardless of who is injured upon impact.

The difficult point about this plea is only whether it can be established in fact. In some cases the argument will be easy. Thus, where B makes a left turn and is struck by A who is traveling in the opposite direction, B will have to bear all the costs of the accident regardless of who is injured in the collision, unless B can introduce a plea that again shifts the balance in his favor.[10] Other cases raise more difficult problems. Nearly all rear-end collisions will be decided in favor of the front car because the paradigm of force is so clearly operative. The driver of the rear car cannot, for example, claim to have the right of way when the front car has stopped at a red light. Yet in some cases the front car could well be held at fault on the ground that it blocked the rear car's right of way, say by a "sudden stop," and these cases may be complicated by some further traffic regulation not taken into account in the

---

been injured, it is clear on causal grounds that he would have to bear the loss. (The case could be complicated if the bearer of the explosives could show that the defendant's servant trespassed against his person. See *infra* chap. IX. But although he could establish the touching, there is doubtless some license for it given that the plaintiff was a passenger on defendant's train.) *Palsgraf,* however, is a difficult case because the injured party was not causally responsible for the harm in any way. When she sued the railroad, she chose the "wrong" defendant, for her better case was against the bearer of the explosives. These "trigger" cases (see generally, Joel Feinberg, Doing and Deserving, 167–73 (1970)) are the hardest to solve because, though the balance favors the plaintiff, it is close indeed. Regardless of its solution, the case does not need a "duty" analysis of the sort given it by Cardozo.

[8] Again there is the possibility of the independent defense of the plaintiff's trespass or his assumption of risk.

[9] See, *e.g.,* Greenman v. Yuba Power Products, Inc., 59 Cal. 2d 57, 27 Cal. Rptr. 697, 377 P.2d 897 (1962).

[10] For instances of such pleas, see *infra,* text at notes 18–26.

setting of the rights of ways, such as one that requires the rear car to maintain a certain minimum distance from the front car. Thus the causal paradigms will not exhaust all possible variations in fact, and are insufficient to set out a *per se* rule for liability even if they can establish a valid plea.[11]

Similar problems will occur, moreover, in collisions at an intersection where there are neither stop signs nor traffic lights. But where state law provides that the first to enter has the right of way, then he will prevail prima facie on the strength of that rule in any action between them, for it will determine which party blocked the right of way of the other; and if the state law provides that when two cars approach the intersection at about the same time, the car to the right has the right of way, then the driver of that car will prevail. If the two rules point in opposite directions, the case will be a difficult one indeed.

The problems of rights of way are also troublesome in cases of accidents at railroad crossings, particularly where an automobile is struck by an oncoming train. Within the framework of the analysis here the crucial question often is who is given the right of way, the train or the car, with the risk of loss being placed prima facie, but only prima facie, upon the party who did not have it. Suppose the crossing is unguarded and the train has the right of way, as is almost always the case.[12] With the assignment of rights

---

[11]Thus the system of staged pleas parallels the negligence system in that it too makes it impossible to lay down any *per se* rule of liability, since each plea in the system is defeasible. That result is achieved today in the negligence law because the concept of "reasonableness" permits innumerable factors to bear on the ultimate issue of defendant's conduct. It thus rejects Holmes's view that judicial standards can be laid down as a *per se* matter in common types of cases. Oliver Wendell Holmes, Jr., *supra* chap. VI, note 5, at 122–24.

[12]These rights of way should, of course, be established on rational and efficient grounds, for the state in the exercise of its proprietary powers should set standards that tend to advance the common welfare. But suppose that it does not; still, it is not for the courts to decide a given case on the ground that rights of way should have been established as the court would have it, for at this point the difference in institutional function precludes the courts from looking to the multitude of factors that properly influence a legislature or traffic department. The argument is made in much these terms by John Rawls, Two Forms of Rules, 64 Philosophical Rev. 3 (1955), where he uses the important distinction between justifying a rule and justifying a practice under it to show that utilitarian considerations are important in the first context if not in the second. It is also reflected in the widespread rejection of the position that statutes are "mere evidence" of the appropriate standard of care in accident cases. See generally William L. Prosser, *supra* chap. VI, note 1, at § 36.

thereby established, there is no reason to make the inquiry, so typical in negligence cases, as to whether the driver took those precautions expected of the reasonable man. Justice Holmes may have been quite unwise in *Baltimore and Ohio R.R. v. Goodman*[13] to suggest that a man should get out of his car to look down the track when he has reason to believe a train may be dangerously near. But the decisive criticism of Holmes's position is not, as Cardozo argued seven years later in *Pokora v. Wabash Ry.*,[14] that Holmes's prescription for safety is unwise because it could well lead to more crossing accidents than it avoids. The question of prudence is beside the point, for Holmes's decision could have rested quite well on the observation that "[the plaintiff] knows that he must stop for the train, not the train stop for him,"[15] which is but another way of saying that the train has the right of way. At that point it is left for the driver of the car to devise whatever strategies he chooses to keep off the tracks when the train is coming, and if life—his life—is at stake, he has every incentive to find appropriate means to achieve that end. The case, of course, does not end necessarily with a showing that the train had the right of way; other safety regulations may still bear on the result. But, given the general theory of strict liability, the presumption created by determining the right of way is not overridden by any kind of showing that the risk taken by the driver when he crossed the tracks was indeed a reasonable one.[16]

The kinds of inquiries demanded in right-of-way cases are no doubt well known to personal injury lawyers, and thus to some extent appear to fit within the framework of negligence law ostensibly used to decide these cases. Indeed, in *The Common Law* Holmes had noted as part of his discussion of negligence that the law of tort could not function if it had to depend solely on the "featureless generality" that holds the defendant to the standard of care of a prudent man under all the circumstances of the case. There is, as he pointed out, a strong pressure on the system to reduce the general standard to specific substandards.

---

[13]275 U.S. 66 (1927).

[14]292 U.S. 98 (1934).

[15]275 U.S. at 69–70.

[16]The alternative view is taken within the negligence system where it is often stated that the assumption of risk must be unreasonable in order for it to be a defense to the action. See *infra* chap. VIII, text at notes 8–10.

Holmes thus approved of the adoption of specific rules of the road, for by their use "the question has been narrowed from the vague one, Was the party negligent? to the precise one, Was he on the right or the left of the road?"[17] But the shift in questions does more than lend precision to the inquiry. It involves the substitution, perhaps unintended, of a strict standard for a reasonableness one. If Holmes wanted only to narrow the inquiry without changing the theory of liability, the appropriate question would be not whether the party is on his side of the road, but, in the event he was not, whether he had nonetheless made a reasonable effort to stay there. The specificity achieved by that question, however, only identifies the paradigm appropriate to the question of "proximate" cause; it does not, as the *Carroll Towing* formula suggests, give specific content to the "featureless generality" of reasonable care in the context of the defense of contributory negligence. Indeed, where the defendant's conduct is no longer in issue, and the prima facie case is established, the plaintiff can be expected to bring forth the same level of effort whether or not the reasonableness requirement is engrafted upon the causal defense, for in both cases the plaintiff will cross over the middle of the road only if his expected benefits exceed his expected costs. As ever, only one's view of fairness should determine the choice of rule, and on that ground the defense should be strict.

It remains now to consider the effect of the defense of plaintiff's use of force upon the plaintiff's prima facie case based upon force. Suppose *A* alleges that *B* hit him, and *B* wishes to plead as his defense that *A* hit him as well, to *A*'s own damage. Here the plea should be accepted as a good, but partial, affirmative defense. *B* sets out a causal relationship between *A*'s own act and the harm he suffers. But he does not rest his case on a causal plea that is entitled to priority over *A*'s causal allegation, because both pleas only invoke forces created independently of each other. At this point, therefore, we get a true case of joint causation,[18] in which the want of a clear priority raises questions about

---

[17]Oliver Wendell Holmes, Jr., *supra* chap. VI, note 5, at 113.

[18]This form of defense is not analyzed in Richard A. Posner, *supra* note 6, where only the cases of strict liability with contributory negligence or with no defense at all are taken into account. Note that a system of strict liability with the defense of contributory negligence can produce odd results that are avoided here. Suppose

the proper apportionment of damages. Within a negligence system the losses must remain where they fall when both parties acted with reasonable care. It is also possible to parallel that result in a system of strict liability by saying that no losses should be shifted unless one party can establish a clear causal priority over the other. Nonetheless that result could well prove unjust, particularly if A drove a heavy car at high speed when B drove a light car at slow speed. Since by assumption only the paradigm of force is involved in the case, it is perhaps best to measure the loss attributable to each by the energy his act released at the time of the collision. The portion of the total damages that A must bear is measured by

$$\frac{M_A V_A^2}{M_A V_A^2 + M_B V_B^2} \qquad \frac{E_A}{E_A + E_B}$$

where M_A is the mass of A's car and V_A is its velocity at the time of impact, and M_B the mass of B's car and V_B its velocity. Likewise B's portion of the loss is measured by

$$\frac{M_B V_B^2}{M_A V_A^2 + M_V V_B^2} \qquad \frac{E_B}{E_A + E_B}$$

If A's portion of the damage is greater than his causal contribution to that total, he should be allowed to recover the difference; and if his portion of the damage is the less, he should be made to pay the difference. The parallel arguments of course apply to B. In neither case do the costs of avoidance play any role in the analysis.

The discussion thus far has considered only those cases that bring into play the four basic paradigms of causation. Yet in the context of traffic accidents it is clear that far more must be taken into account in many cases before the issues of liability and damages can be resolved. In particular special attention must be paid to the statutes that impose duties upon users of the highway. These statutes can take many forms, but since the analysis proceeds in the same way regardless of the specific statutory require-

---

there is a head-on collision in which neither driver is negligent. Under this regime it seems that each will be able to recover for his own injuries, for each will be able to make out the prima facie case, and neither will be able to make out the defense. It is hard to see why that system is attractive when it makes the equities of the case turn on the fortuity of who is injured. That unfortunate result is reached in systems of negligence and contributory negligence, but at least there is no need for two lawsuits to establish the result.

ment, we shall treat but one class of statutes, those which place a maximum speed limit upon automobiles that use the highway.

The speeding statute can be introduced into a case in several different contexts. Thus, in a two-car collision between *A* and *B*, *A* could, as plaintiff, use the familiar pattern "*B* hit *A*" to state his prima facie case. Assume now that none of the causal defenses that operate as complete defenses to the prima facie case is available to *B*. *B* might still be able to rely on the partial defense that *A* struck *B*, causing part of his own damages. Now if *A* were speeding just before the collision took place, *B* should be able to reduce the damages that he otherwise will be required to pay by pleading that either party could have avoided the accident if *A* had not been speeding. At this point notions of *avoidance* are introduced into the scheme of liability to supplement the strict causal notions already taken into account. This notion of avoidance is central to the articulation of the negligence principle, with its persistent question whether the defendant could have avoided the harm to the plaintiff if he had taken the precautions of the reasonable man. But negligence at common law leaves it unclear precisely what specific precautions are to be expected, and the vain attempt to answer that question has only brought forth the inadequate standard of the reasonable man and the complexities of the *Carroll Towing* formula. The statute, however, eliminates that problem in its entirety because it specifies in advance the particular conduct demanded of persons using the public highway.

These statutes are, to be sure, given great respect in the negligence law, particularly jurisdictions which hold that noncompliance with a statute is conclusive proof of negligence.[19] Yet there is no need whatsoever to wed noncompliance with the statute to the theory of negligence. The statute can be pleaded in its own terms as a defense to the plaintiff's prima facie case.

Once the statute is pleaded as a defense, attention must be paid to its precise effect. In some cases the plea based upon the statute will amount to a complete defense because the defendant could prove that all of the harm could have been avoided had the plaintiff complied with the statutory command. The proof of the

---

[19]See the strong statement of Ezra Ripley Thayer, Public Wrong and Private Action, 27 Harv. L. Rev. 317, 319-28 (1914). For a judicial exposition of the negligence *per se* doctrines see Osborne v. McMasters, 40 Minn. 103, 41 N.W. 543 (1889). See generally William L. Prosser, *supra* chap. VI, note 1, at § 36.

avoidance issue, however, might tend to show only that a portion of the damages involved could have been avoided by statutory compliance. At that point, the appropriate solution is to bar the plaintiff's recovery of the avoidable portion of the damages. The rest should be apportioned, as before, on the basis of the formula that allocates damages as a function of the comparative kinetic energies of the two cars, with but one correction: The plaintiff should be treated at the time of the crash as though he drove, not at the speed he did, but at the maximum permissible speed limit, in order to ensure that the excess speed in question is not taken into account twice.

The same strategy can be used in the case where *B* sues *A* after a crash that resulted in part because *A* was speeding. The general pleading rules of minimum sufficiency[20] bar *B* from raising the statutory point in his prima facie case, because he is entitled to recover his damages in full on the strength of the allegation *A* hit *B*. In the second stage of the case, *A* will plead that *B* also hit *A* and then argue for an apportionment of damages by the formula applicable when force alone is in issue. *B* now should be able to plead by way of reply that all or part of the damages could have been avoided if *A* had complied with the speeding statute.

The speeding statute can also be taken into account where the causal paradigm of blocking or interfering with a right of way is raised by the facts of a case. Such a situation is presented, with one small but important modification, by the famous case of *Mahoney v. Beatman*,[21] the facts of which are summarized by Gregory and Kalven in their casebook on torts as follows:

> Plaintiff in that case was driving a Rolls Royce about 60 miles per hour, while it was still daylight, on a gravel-shouldered, two-lane concrete turnpike, with a clear view in both directions. Defendant was approaching in a Nash from the other direction and, turning to speak to somebody in the back seat, permitted the Nash to cross over the middle of the highway into plaintiff's lane. Plaintiff, in order to avoid a head-on collision, pulled the Rolls Royce partly off onto the shoulder so that only his left wheels were on the pavement, and the Nash hit and grazed the Rolls Royce's left-hand front hub cap and spare tire, causing what was estimated as about

[20]The concept holds basically that a party can allege at any stage in the argument only the very minimum necessary for him to achieve all of his remedial objectives. See Richard A. Epstein, *supra* chap. V, note 5, at 577.

[21]110 Conn. 184, 147 Atl. 762 (1929).

$200 damage. The Rolls Royce proceeded for about 125 feet along the road and suddenly turned across the highway, climbed a small bank and hit a tree and stone wall, causing about $5650 additional damage to the car.[22]

On the strength of these facts the trial judge, in a case tried without a jury, held that the plaintiff could recover only the $200 in damage caused by the original impact, and not the $5,650 of damages incurred subsequently when the car ran up the embankment, since the plaintiff's chauffeur had driven the car at an "unreasonable" rate of speed which "hampered" his control over the vehicle after the initial impact. The Connecticut court did not state how the trial judge had determined the "unreasonableness" of the plaintiff's speed, though it is at least possible that he applied the usual negligence standard of reasonableness. We shall treat the case as though the speed limit was set by statute, in order to show the place of statutory requirements in a system of strict liability.[23]

On that assumption, the plaintiff's prima facie case states that the defendant both struck him and blocked his right of way. Given the notions about priority among the paradigms, it is clear that the defendant could not plead only that the plaintiff struck him as well. The problem that remains concerns that portion of the damages both caused by defendant's blocking the road and avoidable by plaintiff's compliance with the statute, where the latter point could be raised as an affirmative defense.[24] In previous

---

[22]Charles O. Gregory & Harry Kalven, Jr., *supra* chap. V, note 2, at 367–68. The references to the clear road and the conversation with the person in the back seat, however material they might be to the law of negligence, play no role in the causal analysis.

[23]This need not have been the case, of course, for most statutes have saving clauses which prohibit driving at unreasonable rates of speed regardless of the stated speed limits. It does not follow that these statutes require us to make a detailed cost-benefit analysis of the cases to which they apply. That requirement could be construed as holding that no person is permitted to drive his car at a speed which might cause him to lose control, regardless of the private benefits obtainable from taking the risks involved. On this view the term "unreasonable speed" simply instructs the finder of fact to use some specific number lower than the stated speed limit to determine the avoidable portion of the damages.

[24]We put to one side the dubious argument that the plaintiff's conduct was the cause of the harm because "but for" his speeding, the accident would not have happened. That analysis applies with equal force to the case where the plaintiff speeded at some earlier time and thus reached the scene of the accident only to be

cases it was possible to assert that, as between blocking and hitting, the former should be treated as decisive on the question of responsibility, on the ground—to take a useful phrase from the Restatement—that the hitting was "dependent" upon the blocking, and not the other way around.[25] Yet no priority can be established between the blocking and the speeding because each proceeded independently of constraints placed upon it by the other. At this point the theory of strict liability finds itself in the same unhappy bind that troubles the law of negligence when the carelessness of both parties is said to contribute to the plaintiff's harm. One could take the traditional common law view, prohibiting the apportionment of damage attributable to the negligence of both parties, and apply it as well to a system where the harm is attributable to the conduct of both. Nonetheless, it is at least possible that the movement toward comparative negligence should influence the allocation decision within a system of strict liability because in both cases it is possible to assert that ultimate distribution of the loss should not turn on the fortuity of which party was injured. In any event, the allocation cannot be conducted under the formulas used in the case of harm produced by joint forces, because the blows as such are no longer the basis of responsibility. Hence the solution is quite arbitrary, though it seems intuitively attractive to conclude with Leon Green that greater weight should be attached to driving on the wrong side of the road.[26]

It is also profitable to consider under these principles the counterclaim that could arise from the case assuming that Beatman's Nash had been damaged. Beatman's prima facie case must rest upon the force paradigm, the Rolls struck the Nash. In turn it

---

struck by the defendant when he, the plaintiff, was traveling under the speed limit. This position, and the countless variations on it, must fail once the "but for" account of causation is rejected. See H. L. A. Hart & A. M. Honoré, Causation in the Law 114–16 (1959). The speeding is material only to the extent that it limits the alternatives to the two drivers immediately before the collision.

[25]See Restatement of Torts 2d, § 441, comment c.

[26]"The inconsiderate handling of a powerful vehicle so as to come into the path of a like rapidly moving machine is of a little deeper dye than the excessive speeding of a machine along a paved country highway." Leon Green, Mahoney v. Beatman: A Study in Proximate Cause, 39 Yale L.J. 532, 541 (1930), reprinted in his Judge and Jury 226, 240 (1930). For criticism of Green's general position, see H. L. A. Hart and A. M. Honoré, *supra* note 24, at 267.

will be met with the plea that the Nash blocked the Rolls's right of way. At this point Beatman could introduce the plea of noncompliance with the statute in his reply. As to unavoidable damages the plea will of course have no effect; as to avoidable damages the question will be whether it is appropriate to apportion damages where there is no way to establish priority between the parties, which on the analysis given above again makes rough apportionment the most attractive solution.

The discussion of the role of statutes in traffic cases also illustrates a general point about the problem of remoteness of damage. The pleading system used here permits a case to be developed in its relevant aspects by an indefinite number of pleas. The general formulas of the tort law that use catchwords like "directness" or "foresight" cannot supply adequate tests for remoteness of damage because they ignore the absolute dependence that the damage question has upon the sequence of pleas needed to establish the defendant's liability. In the case just given, the application of force by two parties, the blocking of a right of way by one of them, and the noncompliance with a statute by the other are all in issue. It is simple folly, even in this comparatively common sort of case, to try to state the applicable rules of liability by an appeal to an undifferentiated notion of proximate cause. Distinctions must be taken first among the varieties of causation, and thereafter between all causal notions, taken together on the one hand, and notions of avoidance on the other. Where each of these distinct elements is raised in its proper sequence, there should be no obstacle to the systematic resolution of the traditional problem of proximate cause in common sense terms.

The availability of defenses based both upon the plaintiff's conduct and the statute thus allows us to account for much of the territory now covered by the plea of contributory negligence, even though neither the moral nor economic interpretations of reasonableness are part of a system of strict liability. As an economic matter, moreover, the system cannot be regarded as any less efficient than that of the current law, once two assumptions common to both are made explicit. First, it is clear that neither the system of strict liability nor the law of negligence imposes any general affirmative duty upon the plaintiff to take steps appropriate to his own self-protection. The maxim, "you take your victim as you find him," has its place in both systems. Second, the general law of negligence does not measure the reasonableness of the plaintiff's conduct by a direct comparison between the two parties to see which is in the better position to avoid the harm. Instead the conduct of the defendant first is measured against an external standard, which is then applied to the plaintiff's conduct. Thus, the negligence rules in their current form could well be construed to hold that the defense of contributory negligence is established if the plaintiff could avoid a $200 accident at the cost of $100, even if the defendant could have avoided that same accident at the cost of, say, $50.[27]

These arguments are not decisive against an economic reformulation of the law of negligence that determines the scope of the duties imposed upon both parties to the accident by a direct comparison of the costs that each must take to avoid it. That approach, however, will run into insuperable difficulties of its own. First, it requires the comparison to be made in advance of the accident when neither party can identify the other. Second, it requires that comparison be made under circumstances where it is difficult, if not impossible, for each person to find out the avoidance costs of the other even if he were fortunate enough to identify him. Third, the system faces the same problem of apportionment that confronts the traditional law of negligence if both parties have failed to take the steps demanded of them. The complexities that stand in the way are so formidable that the system could function only if we were prepared to accept rules of thumb to simplify the required calculations. The first of these rules would be, no doubt, that each party is entitled to make his cost calculations on the assumption that the other party will conform his conduct to some external standard of behavior, and the second that the substance of these standards will be set by statutes of the kind considered above. Yet these two assumptions require the economic theory to abandon the explicit comparative purpose that first motivated its introduction. With economic considerations to one side, the choice between the traditional law of negligence and the alternative system of strict liability should turn upon notions of corrective justice.

[27]See Richard A. Posner, Economic Analysis of Law § 4.3 (1973).

VIII. Assumption of Risk

The set of valid defenses is not limited to those that appeal to causal principles. The first of the noncausal defenses to be examined is that of assumption of risk, or, to be more precise, the plea that the defendant ought not to be responsible for the harm that he inflicted upon the plaintiff because the plaintiff took upon himself the risk of that harm. The rationale for this defense can be stated in one sentence: Whenever the plaintiff assumes the risk of harm inflicted by the defendant, the case presumptively should be treated as though the plaintiff inflicted harm upon himself. Its explication, however, is more complex, as both the scope of the plea and the possible exceptions to it must be determined.

The defense of assumption of risk takes two forms that must be kept distinct because of their different substantive requirements and because of the different kinds of exceptions to which they are subject. The first form of the defense concerns assumption of risk by *consensual* agreement between the plaintiff and defendant, and the second *unilateral* assumption of risk by the plaintiff. The plea of consensual assumption of risk should be governed by the same rules applicable to agreements that do not have safety as their subject matter. Thus, the only parties who should be able to take advantage of the plaintiff's promise to bear the risk are those who are entitled to rely on a like promise in an ordinary contract action. Similarly, an agreement between the plaintiff and a third party for their own mutual benefit will not avail the defendant in a tort action, for he should not be allowed to rest his defense on an agreement that was intended only to allocate certain risks between the parties to it.[1]

When the defense of assumption of risk takes the form of an agreement between the parties, two elements commonly associated with the defense need not be present. First, the plaintiff need not have any specific and distinct perception of the particular risk which he has agreed to assume. It is quite enough that the harm when it occurs falls into the class of accidents the risk of which the plaintiff assumed in his agreement with the defendant. Second, to the extent that we adopt an objective theory of contracts, the plaintiff presumptively will be bound by his manifest assumption of risk even if he does not understand the scope or dimension of the risk that he has undertaken, except perhaps in cases where the defendant knows that he did not mean what he said. Plaintiff's private perceptions of his own acts and their legal significance will count for no more (but no less) than they would in connection with any other agreement to which he is a party. The plea of assumption of risk in this form will in effect provide a contract answer to a tort case.[2]

When the defense is raised in its consensual form it is not correct to say, as is so often said, that the "plaintiff must voluntarily, consciously, and deliberately elect to encounter a known risk."[3]

---

[1]See, *e.g.,* Holgate v. Bleazard, [1917] 1 K.B. 443, where the plaintiff was not held in "default" in a cattle trespass case simply because he had not fenced in his land as he had covenanted to do with his landlord. The breach of duty affected only the parties to the agreement, and could not be seized upon by the defendant to create a duty to him. The same relational aspect of duties appears frequently in defective products cases. The web of warranties among possible codefendants should be of no concern to a plaintiff not party to any of the agreements, but should govern only whatever adjustments need be made among the defendants after the judgment of the plaintiff has been satisfied. See, *e.g.,* Goldberg v. Kollsman Instrument Corp., 12 N.Y.2d 432, 191 N.E.2d 81 (1963), a case in which neither the majority nor the dissent ever quite disentangled the warranty arguments from the causal arguments.

[2]Within the system of strict liability, assumption of risk is a distinct affirmative defense. That view of the defense is not accepted within the law of negligence. "[A]ssumption of risk in the primary sense does not, analytically, describe a defense at all. It is simply a left-handed way of describing a lack of duty," *i.e.,* a duty of care under the law of negligence. Fowler V. Harper & Fleming James, Jr., *supra* chap. VII, note 2, at 1190. It should be noted that as a pleading matter assumption of risk is regarded as an affirmative defense. Fed. Rules Civ. Pro., Rule 8(c).

[3]Francis H. Bohlen, Contributory Negligence, 21 Harv. L. Rev. 233, 246 (1908), reprinted in his Studies, *supra* chap. VI, note 2, at 500, 516.

Nonetheless that description does come close to giving an account of the second, the unilateral, form of the defense. Take the case where a man stops on the street to watch a baseball game, or perhaps a display of fireworks; or the case where he runs in front of a moving train in order to save his own property, or perhaps the life of a small child. In each of these cases it might just be possible to base the defense of assumption of risk on some kind of "implied" agreement between the parties, but the attempt to do so will be both forced and artificial in the vast bulk of cases. Nonetheless it should be possible to make out the defense, subject in principle to exceptions, on the ground that the plaintiff decided that he would take the risk of a known and perceived danger in order to pursue some objective of his own. The defense does not turn in the slightest on some prior course of negotiations between the parties to the case, and therefore can be made out without resort to the rules of contract appropriate to the defense in its first form.

Smith v. Baker nicely illustrates the distinction between the two forms of the defense.[4] The plaintiff was injured in the course of his employment when struck by a stone that had slipped from a crane that was carrying it from one place to another. The plaintiff knew that the crane from time to time slung stones over his head, but he did not have specific knowledge that a stone was being slung at the time of the accident. The House of Lords held that the defense of assumption of risk did not apply, because the plaintiff did not know that this stone was being lifted over his head, much less that he was about to be hit by it.[5] In effect the House of Lords relied exclusively on the unilateral form of the defense, but did not consider whether the defendant could make out the consensual form of that defense on the strength of the employment contract. Lord Bramwell, in dissent, seems to have the better of the argument when he notes that "[t]he plaintiff here thought the pay worth the risk, and did not bargain for compensation if hurt: in effect he undertook the work, with its risks, for the wages and no more."[6] On that view of the case the defense should stand even

---

[4] [1891] A.C. 325. For perceptive comments on the case, see Francis H. Bohlen, Voluntary Assumption of Risk, 20 Harv. L. Rev. 91, 103–06 (1906), reprinted in his Studies, *supra* chap. VI, note 2, at 44.

[5] [1891] A.C. at 335–38, per Lord Halsbury.

[6] [1891] A.C. at 344.

though the plaintiff did not have a conscious appreciation of the risk.[7]

It is often asserted that unilateral assumption of risk should apply if it can be shown that the plaintiff's conduct was unreasonable, where that term is taken to mean that the expected costs of the plaintiff's activities are outweighed by the benefits which he hoped to derive from it.[8] On this view, of course, the defense ceases to be of independent importance because the territory it covers is taken over by the defense of contributory negligence, now made applicable not only to the plaintiff's manner of conduct but also to his choices of action.[9] The incorporation of a reasonableness requirement into the plea of assumption of risk no doubt makes sense within the framework of a negligence system, where the major premise is that no legal consequences ought to attach to conduct which there is no economic or moral reason for the law to change. Nonetheless that limitation upon the defense of assumption of risk has no place whatsoever in a system of strict liability.[10] The question is not whether the conduct of the plaintiff should be changed, but whether his assumption of the risk provides a reason within a system of corrective justice to shift back to the plaintiff the loss now presumptively fastened to the defendant on causal grounds. In our examination of causal pleas, both as they apply to the prima facie case and to the defenses thereto, it was also immaterial that the party who caused the damage acted in a reasonable manner; the questions of reasonableness were for him to decide when he chose to act, not for the courts to pass

[7]The problem in distinguishing the two forms of the defense is raised in a less controversial situation where a spectator at a baseball game is hit by a batted ball. In most cases the consensual form of the defense is applicable, but the cases still speak of the requirement of specific knowledge, often presumed, as if the unilateral form were in issue. See generally, Fowler V. Harper & Fleming James, Jr., *supra* chap. VII, note 2, at 1169–70.

[8]Fowler V. Harper & Fleming James, Jr., *supra* chap. VII, note 2, at 1162.

[9]*Id.* at 162.

[10]"It [the doctrine of assumption of risk] is, and always has been, a kind of plaintiff's strict liability—the other side of the coin of defendant's strict liability." Guido Calabresi & Jon T. Hirschoff, *supra* chap. V, note 4, at 1065. The authors use strict liability to require the court to decide which party is in the better position both to make a cost-benefit analysis of the costs of both accidents and of their prevention, and then to act on it. That meaning is at variance with the traditional causal use of the term. *Id.* at 1060. For criticism, see Richard A. Posner, *supra* chap. VII, note 6, at 213–15.

upon when it made determinations of liability. With assumption of risk in this second sense, exactly the same sort of arguments apply: The prudence of the plaintiff's decision to assume the risk is his own affair, not that of the courts.

The defense of assumption of risk stated in strict form will have the same incentive effects as it will when the reasonableness qualification is inserted, for even without this qualification the plaintiff will have every incentive to make reasonable choices since he must bear the costs of all of his mistakes.[11] The strict form of the plea therefore is consistent with the economic theory, but is by no means required by it. From an administrative point of view, the strict form of the defense seems preferable on economic grounds, as it was with causal defenses, because it tends to reduce both the cost of deciding the truth of the plea and the number of cases for decision.

Before we consider the possible exceptions to the defense of assumption of risk, it is important to note one common set of circumstances insufficient to make out either form of the defense: where the defendant is able to show only that the plaintiff knew that as a matter of course he might be harmed by the defendant's activities.[12] Assumption of risk, like defenses based upon causal notions, must provide a reason that differentiates the defendant's position from the plaintiff's in a manner that resolves the equities between them in favor of the defendant. In the two acceptable forms of the defense, it was the plaintiff *alone* who assumed the risk that the defendant would harm him. In the case of simple knowledge, however, no unique allocation of the risk is possible, for if the plaintiff had knowledge of the risk of harm associated with the defendant's activity, so did the defendant. The plea thus becomes trivial because it leads to the conclusion that both parties assumed the risk of the harm in question since both knew it could occur.

In spite of its weaknesses, this form of the plea has been used

[11]The argument in the text assumes that we judge the efficacy of the defense without making any comparative determination of whether the plaintiff, defendant, or indeed some third party, is best able to take the appropriate steps to avoid the harm. See *supra* chap. VII, text at note 27, for a discussion of the same point in connection with causal defenses.

[12]This version of the plea has, of course, been rejected many times. See, *e.g.,* Smith v. Baker, [1891] A.C. 325, 336–37. See also Leon Green, Assumed Risk as a Defense, 22 La. L. Rev. 77, 80 (1961).

from time to time, with great effect upon the shape of the tort law. Perhaps the most important instance of its use is found in *Fletcher v. Rylands*[13] where Justice Blackburn turns to the notion of assumption of risk in order to explain why traffic accidents should be governed by the law of negligence, and disputes between neighboring landowners by the rules of strict liability. He states:

> Traffic on the highways, whether by land or sea, cannot be conducted without exposing those whose persons or property are near to it to some inevitable risk, and that being so, those who go on the highway, or have their property adjacent to it, may well be held to do so subject to their taking upon themselves the risk of injury from that inevitable danger; and persons who by the licence of the owner pass near to warehouses where goods are being raised or lowered, certainly do so subject to the inevitable risk of accident. In neither case, therefore, can they recover without proof of want of care or skill occasioning the accident; and it is believed that all the cases in which inevitable accident has been held an excuse for what prima facie was a trespass, can be explained on the same principle, viz., that the circumstances were such as to shew that the plaintiff had taken the risk upon himself.[14]

In this passage the plea of assumption of risk does not rest upon the conduct or decision of the plaintiff; it is a fictional device for changing the theory of the case from strict liability to negligence. Plaintiff's assumption of risk is accepted in highway cases without proof and is then made subject to the exception that enables the plaintiff to recover prima facie where he can show that the defendant could have avoided the accident by the exercise of reasonable care. The argument, however, proves too much. The same cavalier treatment of assumption of risk could well lead to the conclusion that the plaintiff assumed the risk of avoidable injuries as well, since it is common knowledge that drivers are often careless. Blackburn continues:

> But there is no ground for saying that the plaintiff here took upon himself any risk arising from the uses to which the defendants should choose to apply their land. He neither knew what these might be, nor could he in any way control the defendants, or hinder their building what reservoirs they liked, and storing up in them what water they pleased, so long as the defendants succeeded

---

[13]1 Exch. 265 (1866), *aff'd sub nom.* Rylands v. Fletcher, 3 H.L. 330 (1868).
[14]1 Exch. at 286.

> in preventing the water which they there brought from interfering with the plaintiff's property.[15]

The point about the plaintiff's lack of knowledge of the defendant's activities cannot be decisive. In the first place, it is probably false, at least in those frequent cases in which the defendant carries on his activities in plain view. Second, if the knowledge alone were regarded as material, then one could in effect acquire a license to harm by giving notice of his intention to undertake activities that could prove dangerous to the plaintiff.

The argument fares no better when Blackburn asserts that the owner of land has neither the power nor the right to interfere with the way in which his neighbor uses his own land. That same conclusion applies with equal force to the defendant's use of the public highways, for while the defendant may not have exclusive use of the road, there is nothing an individual plaintiff could do in advance of an accident to control the conduct of a defendant with whom he shares the public highways. The defense of assumption of risk therefore does not apply to cases where the plaintiff is hurt on the highway for the very reasons that it does not apply to cases of damage to his real property.

There is, however, a proper way to distinguish between highway accidents and suits between land owners that rests on the causal arguments developed in the earlier portion of this essay. The causal paradigm of major importance in cases of damage to land is that of force (apart from the few cases where the plaintiff created an inherently dangerous condition on his land, say, by the storage of explosives). What is crucial, however, is that cases of damage to real property do not call into play with regard to the plaintiff's conduct the complex of statutory rules that govern the use of automobiles on the highway. Thus the highway cases are much more likely to turn on the affirmative defenses based upon these notions of causation and avoidance, all of which tend to blur the firm line between the active defendant and the passive plaintiff so typical in actions for damage for real property. These defenses could well change the outcome of any given case, but they do not—in contrast to the extended notions of assumption of risk—convert theories of strict liability into theories of negligence. The content of the prima facie case remains precisely the

---

[15]*Id.* at 287.

same regardless of the nature of the interest invaded and regardless of the possible defenses to it.

The discussion of assumption of risk in the law of tort does not end with an account of the scope of the defense in either of its two acceptable forms. In accordance with the general rules of pleading it is necessary as well to delineate the subsequent pleas which the plaintiff can make in order to override the defense. At this point it is necessary to distinguish between the two effective forms of the defense, because subsequent pleas which are appropriate to the one may well be inappropriate to the other. The first form of the plea, it should be recalled, was in essence contractual in form. The pleas overriding this defense are those appropriate in contract actions. While it is not possible within the confines of this article to give an exhaustive acccount of the reasons why some bargains (or promises, depending on one's view of consideration) should be respected while others should not, it is nonetheless helpful to mention a few of the common contractual pleas which should form the substance of a plaintiff's reply. For example, it is quite proper to allow the plaintiff to plead either his infancy or his insanity when he assumed the risk in this first sense of the term, once it is conceded that these pleas state valid, though defeasible, defenses to contract actions.[16] It is true that these same pleas were ineffective as affirmative defenses to a cause of action based upon causal paradigms. But there is no inconsistency simply because a given plea is accepted in one context after it has been rejected in another. The plea of infancy or insanity, when raised as a defense to a prima facie case dependent upon causal paradigms, cannot be supported on the ground that the plaintiff chose to deal with, and by implication take advantage of, the defendant, for the prior allegations—here those of the plaintiff's prima facie case—make reference only to the defendant's conduct.[17] Where assumption of risk is used in its consensual sense, it is possible to point to a prior course of dealings between the parties, which should have the same effect upon the allocation of losses between the parties as it does upon any other issue made the subject matter of an agreement.

---

[16]Richard A. Epstein, *supra* chap. V, note 5, at 568–71.

[17]This statement is true even in connection with the paradigms of dangerous conditions. The specification of act or event that is the immediate cause of the harm is immaterial to the statement of the prima facie case, even if it is the act of the plaintiff.

The class of permissible exceptions to the defense of assumption of risk shifts when we consider the second form of that defense, where the plaintiff chooses to expose himself to the risk of harm created by the defendant's activities. At that point the plaintiff can no longer argue that the defendant has taken advantage of either his infancy or his insanity in the course of their dealings—there were none. In this context, the class of insufficient replies includes all those pleas which are insufficient as defenses when raised by the defendant in response to the prima facie case. In addition to infancy and insanity, we should reject the pleas of the plaintiff's use of his best efforts to avoid the harm, and also mistake of fact, because they look not at the relationships between the two parties at or before the time of the accident, but only at the strengths and weaknesses of the plaintiff's condition considered in isolation.

The same logic should apply to the pleas of private necessity and compulsion by a third party. The former should have no effect at all, while the latter should, in view of the theories thus far developed, give the plaintiff a separate cause of action against the third person who compelled him to assume the risk. On this view it is somewhat mistaken to describe the defense as one of "voluntary" assumption of risk, at least to the extent that it is inappropriate to call positive acts performed under such external compulsion "voluntary."[18] As with our discussion of compulsion as a defense, the crucial question here should be not its existence but its source. When its source lies in the act of a stranger, the defense of assumption of risk will not be overridden by a plea of compulsion. The opposite result follows where "voluntariness" is treated as an essential element of the defense. Then the plea fails

---

[18]But see W. Page Keeton, "[A] person's movements are generally considered as voluntary as long as they are accompanied by his volition." Assumption of Risk and the Landowner, 20 Texas L. Rev. 562, 570 (1942). If Keeton's view of the subject is accepted then all actions are voluntary by definition. While it is possible to accept this account, I think it is better to keep the notions of voluntary acts and volitional movements distinct, because it allows for better treatment of actions done by mistake or under compulsion. The view of the subject taken here is adopted in Francis H. Bohlen, *supra* note 4, at 14, 22, reprinted in his Studies, *supra* chap. VI, note 2, at 441, 452–53; H. L. A. Hart & A. M. Honoré, *supra* chap. VII, note 24, at 38–41, 130–31. Observe that the plaintiff will be barred by his assumption of the risk where it was not "voluntary" because he was so compelled by a third party.

regardless of the cause of the compulsion, as attention is implicitly shifted from the relationship between the parties to the plaintiff's personal condition.

There is another exception to this second form of assumption of risk, generally recognized in the case law today, which should be rejected within the framework of a theory of strict liability. It is the plea that the plaintiff was entitled to take the risk because he acted to save a person placed in peril by the defendant's activities. *Eckert v. Long Island R.R.*[19] is the classic case which raises this plea. The plaintiff (or more accurately his decedent) was standing about 50 feet from the train tracks when he saw the defendant's train approach a small child of three or four years of age who was sitting on the tracks unaware of the danger. Convinced that the child was exposed to the threat of serious harm, the plaintiff rushed onto the tracks and threw the child to one side. The train hit the plaintiff, injuring him mortally.

On the important question in the case, that of plaintiff's conduct, the court of appeals distinguished between efforts to save property and those to save life. It held that in the latter case only was it reasonable for the plaintiff to expose himself to harm, where the term reasonable was not used to describe a nice balance between costs and benefits but only to bar recovery where the plaintiff acted in a reckless fashion. On its view of the case, the court held that the jury had been warranted in holding that the plaintiff's own conduct was not a bar to his recovery.

Both the result and the logic of the court's decision are inconsistent with the premises of a system of strict liability. There the plaintiff first alleges that the defendant struck him with the train, causing his death. The defendant's first plea is that the plaintiff assumed the risk of being struck by the train.[20] The requisites of that defense in its unilateral form are satisfied because the plaintiff both knew of the particular hazard that he encountered and chose, for whatever reason, to subject himself to it. The plaintiff then urges in his reply that the action can still be maintained because the plaintiff had a good reason to assume the risk, name-

---

[19]43 N.Y. 502 (1871).

[20]The case could as well be argued on the ground that the plaintiff blocked the defendant's right of way, to which the plaintiff could offer the same plea in avoidance as here.

ly, to rescue a person endangered by the defendant's activities, to which it might be added that the rescue was not only attempted, but also successful.

In spite of the intrinsic worth of the plaintiff's motives, the plea as stated should not be accepted. Like the ineffective pleas considered above, it attempts to shift the balance as between the parties by taking into account only the plaintiff's virtue. In substance it urges only that the plaintiff should be allowed to impose upon the defendant the costs of his own heroism. The plaintiff can escape this objection, with what should be an acceptable reply, by alleging that he provided a benefit to the defendant railroad when he relieved it of the costs of a judgment it otherwise would be required to bear. When the reply takes on that form, it can be made out only if the child would have been injured by the railroad under circumstances in which it could be held responsible. Under this approach, there is no longer any need to distinguish the saving of life from the saving of property, because the difference between the two cases is fully taken into account in the valuation of the benefit conferred upon the defendant.

It remains to be considered whether the plaintiff could have recovered from the railroad if he had escaped uninjured after saving the child from harm for which the railroad otherwise could have been held responsible. The point is by no means an easy one, because it requires a venture into the unhappy law of restitution, which in its different interpretations admits of both answers.[21] It is at least reasonable to argue that a plaintiff here should be allowed to recover an amount equal to what he saved the railroad in its time of necessity whether or not he himself is harmed. The economic point is that he should be put into a position where he will bear all costs, including those which are contingent, and collect all benefits, in order to create incentives that might help him make the correct decision about whether to attempt the rescue.

This solution is most uneasy, though not clearly wrong. In the first place, it is hard to have faith that any economic calculations will be made regardless of the rule in crisis situations, or that if made, they will be properly made.[22] Again, in all of these cases it

---

[21] The problem is not confronted in terms by the Restatement of Restitution, where sections 112–17 come closest to the actual problem.

[22] Nonetheless, an early attempt to analyze the concept of negligence in cost-

is easy to argue that the plaintiff acted out of benevolence and not self-interest, making it possible to treat the plaintiff's act as gratuitous. If gratuitous consensual relationships set the standard for recovery, the plaintiff could recover only for his actual loss, if indeed he could recover anything at all. There is not much hard ground to support one rule over the other, but I think that it is proper to compensate the plaintiff only in cases of his actual loss, and then only to the extent that the railroad received a benefit. Given that it was not shown that the railroad would have been responsible for the harm to the child, the plaintiff in *Eckert* is not entitled to recovery under the tort theories developed here.[23]

There are, of course, pleas available to the plaintiff which are sufficient to override the defense of unilateral assumption of risk. The most important of these, and the one to be considered here, concerns the case where the plaintiff assumes the risk because the defendant has forced him either to take the risk of harm or to abandon the enjoyment of his property.

The general point can be first illustrated in connection with rights of way. Suppose the defendant obstructs the plaintiff's right of way in a manner that makes it unsafe for him to use it, and the plaintiff uses it anyway. The plaintiff chose to subject himself to a known and perceived risk created by the defendant in order to obtain some end of his own. Nonetheless the plaintiff should not be barred by the plea of assumption of risk, not because there is no assumption in fact, but because he can give a reason why it should not be dispositive of the merits of the case: The defendant forced the plaintiff either to take the risk or to

---

benefit terms used these rescue cases to illustrate the general proposition even though they do not lend themselves to that sort of calculation to the same extent as more routine accident cases. Henry T. Terry, Negligence, 29 Harv. L. Rev. 40, 40–44 (1915).

[23]The last problem raised by this situation concerns the possible action of the rescuer against the child, when the railroad would not have been responsible to the child in the event that it had been hurt. The rescuer has no traditional tort action against the child, because the child in no way harmed him (the paradigm of dangerous conditions being quite farfetched). As a straight matter of restitution, the rescuer could argue that he should recover for his injuries given the benefit he conferred on the child in the time of its necessity. He may be met with the plea that he meant his rescue to be a gift to the child. Even so it is possible to argue that he should be allowed to recover his expenses, including the costs of his injuries, up to the value that he provided to the child. The Restatement of Restitution, however, tends to deny recovery in these cases where the rescuer does not have a specific intention to charge. Sections 113–17.

abandon his right of way.[24] The initial distribution of property rights means that the defendant is no longer entitled to present the plaintiff with a "take it or leave it" option.[25] Since the right of way belongs to the plaintiff, prima facie he should be entitled as against the person who obstructs it to use it as though it were unimpaired.[26]

The acceptance of that plea does not necessarily end the case. The defendant may have open to him a rejoinder at the fourth stage of argument that shifts the loss back to the plaintiff. One such rejoinder, consistent with the principles of strict liability, is that the plaintiff did not choose the course of action that allowed him to achieve his private objective—safe passage through the obstruction—with the greatest safety to himself and at the least possible cost to the defendant. The plea works as a complete defense in the event that the best alternative use of the right of way assured passage in complete safety, and as a partial defense in the event that it could only have reduced the damages in question. The plea does not make any appeal to notions of balancing or

---

[24]The same result is achieved in a negligence system by putting a gloss on the concept of contributory negligence. "[T]he plaintiff may not be required to surrender a valuable right or privilege merely because the defendant's conduct threatens him with what would otherwise be an unreasonable risk." William L. Prosser, *supra* chap. VI, note 1, at 425.

[25]See Fowler V. Harper & Fleming James, Jr., *supra* chap. VII, note 2, at 1163–64, 1174–75, for a clear exposition of a position that they do not support.

[26]There are, of course, other variations of the plea that could well be accepted. For example, suppose the plaintiff is injured when he slips on ice that the defendant is under a statutory obligation to remove. Where the plaintiff sees the ice, and continues to use the path, the defense of assumption of risk can be used. It could well be overridden by the plea that the plaintiff, say a postman, is himself under a duty to the defendant to deliver the mail that required him to take the risk in question, even if the plaintiff did not in fact provide any benefit on the particular occasion. That position was rejected in Paubel v. Hitz, 339 Mo. 274, 96 S.W.2d 369 (1936), but the decision has been subject to forceful criticism even within the negligence framework. "Isn't it also politic to recognize a cause of action accruing to postmen injured while reasonably brooking minor hazards to deliver mail, a cause of action against addressees who have not used reasonable care to eliminate those hazards." Clarence Morris, Morris on Torts 232 (1953). The court in *Paubel* contrasted the case against private landowners with the case against public utilities that operated facilities from which they had no right to exclude the plaintiff. 339 Mo. at 282, 96 S.W.2d at 373. That case clearly allows the plaintiff to make use of the reply developed in the text, because the plaintiff is no longer faced with a take-it-or-leave-it option. But it does foreclose the extension of the reply to this case, particularly where the defendant did not manifest any intention of keeping the postman off his premises.

reasonableness; instead it acknowledges that the plaintiff's interest is entitled to complete priority, but allows the defendant to show how the plaintiff's injuries could have been reduced or eliminated even if the priority had been strictly observed. There is, morover, a second form of this rejoinder that probably should be accepted even though it does not respect the complete priority of the plaintiff's claims. It allows the defendant to plead that the plaintiff could have avoided the harm at little or no loss or inconvenience to himself, as for example by taking a quick step to the right to get around an obstruction that the defendant placed upon the path.[27]

The plea has its attractions, especially for those who believe that cost-benefit analysis should dominate the law of tort. But nonetheless the result is an unhappy one. First, it enables the defendant to impose costs upon the plaintiff without compensation. Second, it means that a question of degree—how little an inconvenience is little enough?—will be allowed to decide the question of kind—should the plaintiff be able to recover from the defendant? These unhappy aspects are sufficient in my judgment to limit the scope of the plea, but not to eliminate it altogether. It should be enough for the plaintiff to show that he believed that the alternative involved substantial costs that he would have had to bear. The cases tend to support this approach. The most famous of them allowed the plaintiff to recover against the plea of assumption of risk when he used the only entrance to his land to take his horses onto the public way after his path had been obstructed by the activities of the defendant.[28] Administrative im-

[27]See Frelick v. Homeopathic Hospital Ass'n of Delaware, 51 Del. 568, 150 A.2d 17 (1959), where the court held that a plaintiff who at night tripped over a chain stretched over a corner of a parking lot could not recover for her injuries when she knew of the location of the chain and could have avoided it by taking a somewhat longer, but well-lighted, path. The court held that she was guilty of contributory negligence as a matter of law. The case could have turned as well on the plea of assumption of risk, subject to both the reply and rejoinder in the text. Indeed, the case is an easy one because the plaintiff was on the defendant's property as its visitor. Thus it is possible to decide the case without reaching the reply, because plaintiff has no proprietary right of her own.

[28]Clayards v. Dethick, 12 Q.B. 439, 116 Eng. Rep. 932 (1848). The major critic of the case is Lord Bramwell, whose position is in essence that the plaintiff should abandon her right and then bring an action for her loss. His position presupposes a faith in the effectiveness of legal machinery that most of us do not share. For criticism of Bramwell's position see Francis H. Bohlen, *supra* note 4, at 102–03, reprinted in his Studies, *supra* chap. VI, note 2, at 482.

perfections represent the weakest acceptable reasons upon which to base the substantive rules of tort law, and they should be allowed, grudgingly, to operate to create imperfect solutions only in those *de minimis* situations of the sort contemplated by this rejoinder.

Neither of these pleas need necessarily close the case. In principle it is possible for the plaintiff in the fifth stage of the argument, his surrejoinder, to again reestablish a balance in his favor. The plea appropriate in this context takes the form: The plaintiff did all in his power to avoid unnecessary harm to himself as he made his way across the obstruction created by the defendant. The plea is vital to the law because it implies that the defendant will no longer be able to hold the plaintiff to a strict standard of conduct now that his own conduct has placed the plaintiff in a bind from which he seeks to escape. In effect the plea extends the maxim "you take your victim as you find him" from the case of physical frailties to which it usually refers to all aspects of the plaintiff's behavior. The substantive standard does not ask what the reasonable man is apt to do in this situation, for now it does seem unfair to allow the defendant to hold the plaintiff whom he has placed in a bind to a standard of conduct that he cannot in fact meet. The shift must be to the wholly subjective position, one that allows the plaintiff to show how all of his personal weaknesses and defects, whether they stem from infancy, insanity, stupidity, awkwardness, blindness, or whatever, have affected both his decision to act and the manner of his conduct. There is still no reason to follow the law of negligence by recognizing some defects while disregarding others. In effect all the matters that concern the plaintiff's personal strengths and weaknesses held immaterial at all previous stages of the argument now count, not as ultimate issues, but as evidence relevant to the plaintiff's good faith effort to extricate himself from the bind in which the defendant placed him. The reasonable man standard should be of importance only on questions of proof, for the plaintiff could well be asked to explain why he behaved as no ordinary man would choose to do. The staged system of pleadings may require us to extend the argument to five stages before the subjective element is taken into account, but it does enable us to explain the common sense pull towards both strict and subjective theories of responsibility recognized but not systematized in the common law of torts.

This exception to the defense of assumption of risk is not

111

restricted to cases which involve only rights of way. It is also involved in cases of the use and possession of real estate, where it is raised in connection with the maxim that it is no defense that the plaintiff came to the nuisance.[29]

Suppose a farmer decides to plant his crops close to the edge of his property line where they could be burned by sparks emitted from a nearby railroad train. If the crops are indeed burned, there is no doubt that the railroad can make out the defense of unilateral assumption of risk. The case is not one of simple knowledge of the chance that the farmer's crops will be destroyed, for he planted them in a position that increased his exposure to property damage. The hard question raised by the case concerns the availability of the above exception to the defense.

From an economic point of view, it could be argued that, assuming transaction costs between the parties are high, the defense of assumption of risk should be complete where the farmer can avoid the crop damage at a lower cost than the railroad, say by making a different use of his land.[30] That position, however, requires the farmer to forgo both the use of his land and compensation for his resulting loss, and must be rejected because of its inadequate solution to the problem of corrective justice even if it promotes an efficient use of resources. The railroad could not take or retain possession of the farmer's land with the plea that it could make better use of it, even if transaction costs were high enough to preclude a consensual arrangement. The enjoyment of a past windfall does not create the right to enjoy one in the future, and in the normal case the railroad could not continue in possession of the land in question if the applicable statute of limitations had not run.[31] The exception to the plea of assumption of risk similarly prevents the railroad from acquiring an easement to cause damage to the farmer's land by first making an efficient use of its own.[32] The point here is not only that we

---

[29]See, *e.g.,* Sturges v. Bridgman, 11 Ch. D. 852 (1879). See generally Robert C. Ellickson, Alternatives to Zoning: Covenants, Nuisance Rules, and Fines as Land Use Controls, 40 U. Chi. L. Rev. 681, 758–61 (1973).

[30]Richard A. Posner, *supra* chap. VII, note 6, at 206–07.

[31]See generally Robert C. Ellickson, *supra* note 29, at 728.

[32]The same kind of issue is raised in Fontainebleau Hotel Corp. v. Forty-Five Twenty-Five, Inc., 114 So. 2d 357 (Fla. App. 1959). The plaintiff sought to enjoin the construction of a fourteen story addition to the defendant's hotel. The plain-

wish to encourage voluntary transactions where possible.[33] We also wish to vindicate the initial assignment of property rights in favor of the farmer, and that vindication requires at a minimum that he receive compensation for the loss of his interest (whether for use or possession) even if the railroad has achieved by unilateral action an efficient allocation of resources too costly to reach by consensual means.[34]

The case need not end even after this exception to the defense of unilateral assumption of risk is incorporated into the law. Suppose the plaintiff decides to develop his land where the prospect of harm in question is certain, or at least imminent; it does seem unfair to require the railroad to pay for crops whose only value to the farmer lies in their near-certain destruction. Once that plea is allowed, however, the farmer should in turn be permitted, as in the case of rights of way, to plead that he believed in good faith that the danger in question was neither imminent nor certain. The good faith requirement precludes the farmer's use of blackmail threats, and it prevents as well the railroad from holding the farmer to a standard of judgment that is not his. Given that the farmer and the railroad are permanent neighbors, it might well be

---

tiff had developed a swimming area on his own land in a position where it would lie in the shadows of the new structure each afternoon in the winter months, and wanted an injunction to prevent the loss in value associated with the loss of light. The court, per curiam, denied the injunction. Once it was decided, as was undoubtedly the case under Florida law, that "adjoining landowners have an equal right under the law to build to the line of their respective tracts and such height desired by them," the plaintiff by his own unilateral action cannot acquire in effect a restrictive covenant over the defendant's land which will prevent construction above a certain height. For a different view, see Robert C. Ellickson, *supra* note 29, at 756–57.

The court leaves open the question whether the height restriction could be imposed by legislation, but given the analysis here, it follows that such legislation (no matter how often passed) raises serious if not insurmountable questions of taking without compensation. The point becomes particularly clear in instances where cities in effect sell air rights that they previously have zoned away. See *id.* at 703.

[33]See Richard A. Posner, *supra* chap. VII, note 27, at § 4.1.

[34]Where a pure economic approach is taken, the question of compensation to the plaintiff is material only insofar as it affects the amount that the plaintiff will spend in order to take precautions to protect himself. See Richard A. Posner, *supra* chap. VII, note 27, at 78 n.3. That point apart, "[i]t is thus essential that the defendant be made to pay damages and that they be equal to the plaintiff's loss. But that the damages are paid *to the plaintiff* is, from an economic standpoint, a detail. It is payment *by the defendant* that creates incentives for more efficient resource use." *Id.* at 78.

difficult for the farmer to make out the plea if the railroad had given him notice of the dangers that its operations presented to nearby crops. So unless further steps are taken, the law will have to allow the railroad, after notice, to acquire an interest in the farmer's land provided it conducted its own operations in an efficient manner, or in the alternative to permit the farmer to raise crops that he knows he will never harvest.

Once the prospect of harm, then, is either imminent or certain, there will be no adequate solution to the case if damages after the loss are the only possible remedy. Some form of anticipatory relief is clearly needed. The possible permutations are many, but it will be sufficient for our purposes to consider four major variations.[35]

1. The farmer may enjoin the operations of the railroad, and need not pay for the injunction.

2. The farmer may enjoin the operations of the railroad, but only on condition that he pay the costs imposed on the railroad by the injunction.[36]

3. The railroad may continue its operations as before, but only on condition that it pay the farmer permanent damages for the loss of the use of its land.

4. The railroad may continue its operations as before, and has to pay neither permanent damages at the outset nor actual damages should crops be destroyed.

With these four alternatives it is possible in principle to separate the question of the use of the disputed interest in land from the question of who shall receive the value derived from its use. Thus if it is better to have the farmer grow his crops, so that only the first and second alternatives are in issue, the initial assignment of property rights requires that he need not pay the railroad for the retention of that which he already owns.[37] On the other hand, if

---

[35]See, for discussion of these variations, Guido Calabresi & A. Douglas Melamed, Property Rules, Liability Rules and Inalienability: One View of the Cathedral, 85 Harv. L. Rev. 1089, 1115–24 (1972); Robert C. Ellickson, *supra* note 29, at 738–48; Frank I. Michelman, Pollution as a Tort: A Non-Accidental Perspective on Calabresi's Costs, 80 Yale L.J. 647, 666–86 (1971).

[36]Spur Industries, Inc. v. Del E. Webb Development Co., 108 Ariz. 178, 494 P.2d 700 (1972), is an instance of a case in which the court imposed this sort of a solution.

[37]Here that assignment of rights is based upon the causal arguments that established the farmer's prima facie case on the ground that the growing of the crops is in itself not a harm to the railroad while their destruction is clearly a harm to him. See *supra* chap. III, pp. 19–21.

the railroad is allowed to continue its operations as before, that judgment restricts us to the third and fourth alternatives, but does not tell us whether the railroad must pay for the privilege, whether, in other words, it can force a simple taking or only an exchange. That last question too is decided on the strength of the initial assignment of property rights. Since the railroad seeks a shift in that assignment, at the very least it must pay for it, making the third alternative the only acceptable one.

The original assignment of property rights, then, requires us to select between two alternatives: that which gives the farmer his injunction, and that which requires him to settle for permanent damages.[38] Where consensual arrangements are out of the question, and railroading the more valuable activity, the economic arguments from efficiency should in principle require the farmer to settle for damages in the case. That result, however, must be an uneasy one, for it allows the railroad at its own option to convert the plaintiff's application for an injunction into a suit for the inverse condemnation of an interest in the farmer's land.[39] If the public use language in the governing law is broad enough to permit condemnation by railroads, inverse condemnation should create no particular difficulties. If the condemnation provisions, however, are more restrictive, the problems are acute because the court will, if it denies the farmer's application for an injunction, in effect allow a private party to take an interest in his land under circumstances in which it would be impermissible for the government to do the same thing.

To put the point another way, the rules that govern the plaintiff's case for the injunction should be precisely those which cover the case of inadvertent encroachment of one man's building upon the land of another, for the nuisance and trespass cases should be treated alike. In the encroachment cases the plaintiff is always entitled to damages and may be able to obtain injunctive relief as well once the court makes a balance of the "equities" in the case.[40] The balance that is required, moreover, is not simply one

[38]See, for a discussion of the possible remedies, Robert C. Ellickson, *supra* note 29, at 738–48.

[39]See, *e.g.,* Boomer v. Atlantic Cement Co., 26 N.Y.2d 219, 257 N.E.2d 870 (1970), where the dissent rests its case against an award of permanent damages on the inverse condemnation argument.

[40]See generally 6A American Law of Property § 28.17 (1954); Henry L. McClintock, Discretion to Deny Injunction Against Trespass and Nuisance, 12 Minn. L. Rev. 565 (1928).

of the relative costs and benefits to parties. There both is, and should be, a greater interest "in the protection of individual rights than in the profits to inure to individuals by the invasion of those rights."[41] Thus the defendant may be required in the encroachment case to remove structures that should be allowed to remain if economic arguments were alone material.[42] This same approach should apply as well to the case between the railroad and the farmer, for here too maximization of social wealth is not the only concern of the law. The plaintiff may well be required to change his course of conduct. If so, he should receive compensation for it because of the loss of proprietary rights which that alteration entails.

[41]McCleery v. Highland Boy Gold Min. Co., 140 Fed. 951, 952 (1904).

[42]Some courts have held that the argument against private eminent domain requires that an injunction be issued as a matter of course once the invasion of the proprietary interest is conceded. See, *e.g.,* Holman v. Athens Empire Laundry Co., 149 Ga. 345, 100 S.E. 207 (1919).

IX. Plaintiff's Trespass

The last defense we shall examine concerns cases in which the plaintiff has prima facie trespassed against the defendant's person or property. The arguments here proceed in much the same manner regardless of the nature of the interests invaded, so the problem will be considered mainly in connection with trespass to real property, since it is in this connection that most of the legal issues arise. A few features of the defense must first be noted. First, the plea is relational, and the "his" important, for the defendant cannot assert that the plaintiff was injured while on the land of a stranger;[1] such an entry would be a matter of concern only between the plaintiff and the third party.[2] Nor is the plea based upon causal considerations, because the plaintiff is barred even if none of the causal paradigms considered above are applicable.[3] Finally, the plea is not embraced by either form of assumption of risk, for neither agreement between the parties nor the plaintiff's perception of the danger is required to make out the defense.

The plea, the plaintiff entered the defendant's land, sets out an independent defense designed to vindicate the proprietary interests that are legally protected when one person enters the land

---

[1]See, *e.g.,* Humphrey v. Twin State G. & E. Co., 100 Vt. 414, 139 Atl. 440 (1927); William L. Prosser, *supra* chap. VI, note 1, at 359. Note that those, like family or servants, who can be identified with the owner will be able to claim the benefit of the plea.

[2]See *supra,* text at chap. V, note 8.

[3]But see Hynes v. New York Central R.R. Co., 231 N.Y. 229, 131 N.E. 898 (1921). The plaintiff (more accurately, his decedent) stood on a makeshift diving board attached to defendant's right of way, but over a public river. He was killed when high tension wires erected by the defendant fell on him. The plaintiff was, or at least could be viewed, as a trespasser as against the railroad, but the court held that he could recover, giving as one ground for its decision that there was no causal connection between the decedent's trespass and his death. 231 N.Y. at 234-35, 131 N.E. at 899-900.

of the other. Suppose the plaintiff either had damaged the real estate in question or had sought to retain permanent possession of it. In either case the defendant is prima facie entitled under the theory of strict liability to recover damages or possession, or both, without having to show either the plaintiff's negligence or intent. "You entered my land," or "you damaged it," are both prima facie cases that vindicate the defendant's interest in the exclusive possession of his land. If the trespass action is strict when the plaintiff seeks to protect his possession of land,[4] then the defense should—as with both causal pleas and assumption of risk—assume a strict form as well when the defendant wishes to protect his rights of exclusive use. The claims of exclusive possession would count for nothing if they did not serve as an independent ground to shift back to the plaintiff the risk of accidents that occurred on defendant's land, when prima facie he had no business being there at all.

The problem of the plaintiff's entry upon the defendant's land cannot receive such a summary treatment within the law of negligence. It has been described as an "imperfect area" of negligence law[5] because the proprietary thrust of the defendant's claim has been but awkwardly harmonized with the general reasonableness requirements of the law of negligence. One source of difficulty stems from the general requirements of the prima facie case for trespass to land. At common law trespass to land remained one of the last strongholds of strict liability, a clear anachronism once it was held that trespass to the person required proof of negligence or intent. The reasons why the distinction is plausible, though erroneous, have been discussed above, but in any event they are not of importance here. The crucial point to note is that where the tort is no longer treated as strict, then it is difficult as well to accept the defense in its strict form. Let the defendant plead only that the plaintiff has entered his land, and he has said nothing to excite the interest of the court. At best the plaintiff is an "innocent" trespasser[6]—one guilty of no wrong—and therefore not required

---

[4]The argument is noted in Fowler V. Harper & Fleming James, Jr., *supra* chap. VII, note 2, at 1438 n.21, but they give no clear reason why they reject it, save their general reliance on negligence theory.

[5]Charles O. Gregory & Harry Kalven, Jr., *supra* chap. V, note 2, at 370.

[6]Fowler V. Harper & Fleming James, Jr., *supra* chap. VII, note 2, at 1439 & n.25; Videan v. British Transport Commission [1963] 2 Q.B. 650, 663.

to forfeit any of the protection that the law of negligence affords injured plaintiffs in the general case.

The second problem follows quickly from the first. The general formulas of "reasonable foresight" thought to determine the scope of the defendant's duty of care in the general negligence case do not, as was argued quite persuasively in *Rowland v. Christian,*[7] appear to admit of any principled exception in connection with plaintiffs who enter the defendant's premises. It is an undeniable proposition that some people are in the habit of using the premises of others for their own exclusive benefit.[8] Accordingly, the event ought to fall easy prey to the test of reasonable foresight, particularly given the strained and expansive constructions that test receives in order to assure plaintiff's recovery when only the question of remoteness of damage is at stake. The foresight test, then, works in favor of the trespassing plaintiff, making it necessary to find reasons why the defendant did *not* owe this plaintiff a duty of care.[9] The conventional common law technique on this point, and one still influential today, is to revert to the original premise that the plaintiff cannot use his own wrong

[7]69 Cal. 2d 108, 112–13, 70 Cal. Rptr. 97, 443 P.2d 561 (1968). The California Supreme Court relied on the famous statement of the scope of the duty of care by Brett, M.R., in Heaven v. Pender: "whenever one person is by circumstances placed in such a position with regard to another that every one of ordinary sense who did think would at once recognise that if he did not use ordinary care and skill in his own conduct with regard to those circumstances he could cause danger of injury to the person or property of the other, a duty arises to use ordinary care and skill to avoid such danger." 11 Q.B.D. 503, 509 (1883). That passage is also used by Harper and James as the basis of their attack on the special rules for trespassers, Fowler V. Harper & Fleming James, Jr., *supra* chap. VII, note 2, at 1430, even though it was dissented from by Cotton, L.J. and Bowen, L.J. who both found the proposition "unnecessarily broad." Brett, M.R. (as Lord Esher, M.R.), moreover, retreated from the general principle in Le Lievre v. Gould, [1893] 1 Q.B. 491, 497, when he held that the defendant surveyor was not liable in negligence after he had carelessly prepared papers upon which the plaintiff had relied because there was no duty of care. *Heaven v. Pender* was expressly distinguished. For powerful criticism of his dictum in *Heaven v. Pender,* see Abraham Harari, The Place of Negligence in the Law of Tort 111–14 (1962).

[8]But see Videan v. British Transport Commission, [1963] 2 Q.B. 650. "The true principle is this: In the ordinary way the duty to use reasonable care extends to all persons lawfully on the land, but it does not extend to trespassers, for the simple reason that he cannot ordinarily be expected to foresee the presence of a trespasser." *Id.* at 665–66, per Denning, M.R. See for a different view of the problem the judgment of Pearson, L.J., [1963] 2 Q.B. at 676, and Commissioners for Railways v. Quinlan, [1964] A.C. 1054.

[9]Rowland v. Christian, 69 Cal. 2d 108, 112–13, 70 Cal. Rptr. 97, 443 P.2d 561 (1968).

to create a duty of care in his own favor.[10] That argument is decisive within a system of strict liability, because the plaintiff's prima facie case makes only causal allegations, and contains no reference to any duty of care. But it is weaker by far in a negligence context, where the duty of care is made part of the law before the plaintiff's trespass is introduced as an affirmative defense. Since the trespass is "innocent," or at best "technical," there is no strong reason to disregard the general rule on the duty of care in this particular context. At best it could be urged that the level of duty should be lowered because "while consciously trespassing, [trespassers] do not generally expect land to be prepared for their own safety and realize they must keep a lookout for their own protection."[11] Yet even here the argument is not decisive, but circular, because the level of expectation said to determine the rule rests in large measure upon what the rule is. If the straight negligence approach applied, then trespassers would quickly learn that their presence must be anticipated and provided for, and their expectations would quickly change in a way that eliminated any basis for the lower standard. Rules determine expectations as much as expectations determine rules.

The conceptual purification of the law of negligence has led quite naturally to a retreat from the rule that landowners owed trespassers no duty of care, but that retreat is by no means complete. The second Restatement of Torts, more influential in this area than in perhaps any other, makes it clear at the outset that plaintiff trespasser, whatever his rights, is not entitled to the full protection of the law of negligence.[12] And the exceptions to the general rule reflect only the unhappy compromises needed to account for the position of the trespassing plaintiff in the current law. Thus one important exception in the Restatement[13] provides that the defendant is required to show reasonable care for the benefit of a trespassing plaintiff whenever he creates or maintains a "highly dangerous artificial condition" upon his own land that

[10]Commissioners for Railways v. Quinlan, [1964] A.C. 1054, 1085–86.

[11]Fowler V. Harper & Fleming James, Jr., *supra* chap. VII, note 2, at 1444. Their remark suggests that there might be a difference in the duty owed to persons who knew they were trespassing and those who did not. None, however, has developed in the law. See also Restatement, Torts 2d, § 335, comment f.

[12]Restatement of Torts 2d, § 333.

[13]*Id.* at § 335. See also the closely related provisions of § 334.

is likely to cause death or serious bodily harm to "constant" trespassers who use only a limited area of his land, provided the trespassers cannot be expected to discover the dangerous condition in question. There is clearly more at stake here than the *Carroll Towing* formula. Certain set features—constant trespasses, highly dangerous activities, limited area of land, death or bodily harm—which amount at most to evidence of the reasonableness of the risk are transformed into threshold requirements that must be satisfied before the general question of defendant's negligence can even be confronted.

One important feature of the rule limits defendant's duty toward the plaintiff to cases where the defendant has "created or maintained" the dangerous condition that caused the harm. That requirement, as the comments in the Restatement point out, is difficult to justify within the framework of the law of negligence.[14] The expected benefits from specific precautions could exceed, and by a wide margin, the costs needed to secure them even where the dangerous conditions are natural in origin. Thus precautions with respect to natural hazards could be required of the defendant on a case-by-case basis exactly as if he had created the condition in question.[15]

Yet the distinction between dangerous conditions created by natural causes and those created by the defendant makes perfectly good sense when the problem is viewed in the context of a theory of strict liability. Whenever the dangerous conditions are created by natural forces, the plaintiff will be unable to recover from the defendant, whether or not he entered the defendant's land before the accident took place, because he cannot satisfy the act requirement of the tort law: Ownership per se is not an act of the defendant.[16] Hence the case simply raises in connection with real prop-

[14]*Id.* at § 335, comment b. See also William L. Prosser, Trespassing Children, 47 Calif. L. Rev. 427, 446 (1959).

[15]The general rule that creates the limited duty of care is qualified by a provision that says that no such duty exists where the artificial conditions duplicate those of nature, even if dangerous. See Fowler V. Harper & Fleming James, Jr., *supra* chap. VII, note 2, at 1452. That rule does not make good sense if the act requirement is taken seriously, but it does make sense where the emphasis is placed on the sort of hazards of which the plaintiff ought to take special note.

[16]Restatement of Torts 2d, § 363. Under current law, ownership *per se* will be sufficient to create a prima facie case in tort where the defendant owns trees, even when naturally grown, that threaten to topple and injure users of the public high-

erty the problem of the good Samaritan that has already been encountered in the context of the rescue cases.[17] Given the no-liability resolution of the good Samaritan case, it follows that there is no reason to impose liability simply because the defendant was better able to prevent the plaintiff's harm than the plaintiff himself. There is no prima facie case and no need to consider possible affirmative defenses that otherwise might be available to the defendant.

On the other hand, where the defendant has harmed the plaintiff there is a good prima facie case regardless of whether the defendant exercised reasonable care. At this point, the plaintiff's entrance on the defendant's land is crucial because it forms the basis for a sufficient affirmative defense. This kind of logic is no doubt implicit in the Restatement's position, even though it is obscured by its devotion to the negligence principle. Yet once negligence is rejected as the basis for liability in the general case, there is no reason to treat it as an unattained ideal in the specific context of plaintiff's trespass.

The requirement of the "constant" trespass upon the limited area raises problems of its own. Within the traditional law, the use of the limited area, say a path, was important in two respects. First, it counted as evidence on the question of whether a license in fact could be implied on the basis of all the circumstances of the case,[18] a possibility ruled out here because it is conceded that the constant users of the path are indeed trespassers. Second, the constant—and adverse—use of the path could support a finding that a right of way was acquired by prescription. Yet that line too is ruled out because the plaintiff is conceded to be a trespasser

---

ways in urban areas. William L. Prosser, *supra* chap. VI, note 1, at 355–56. The result has been defended on economic grounds. Robert C. Ellickson, *supra* chap. VIII, note 29, at 727–28. Given the position above, this result is wrong as a matter of tort theory because of the affirmative obligations it imposes. The better solution is to allow the city at its own expense to make the tree safe, after perhaps imposing only the duty to inspect upon the owner. The case is one that allows the public purpose to be accomplished by a forced exchange instead of a simple taking. Where the benefit to be derived works in favor of both the landowner and the public, it might be proper to apportion the expense between them.

[17]Fowler V. Harper & Fleming James, Jr., *supra* chap. VII, note 2, at 1452.

[18]See *id.* at § 27.7 for a discussion of the ways in which the reclassifications of trespassers take place, and the unfortunate consequences of the use of fictions in the process. One can agree with those remarks even if he defends the older conceptions of liability.

whom the defendant could, if he chose, exclude from the use of his land, no matter what the plaintiff wanted to do. In effect, therefore, the requirement of the Restatement implies that in a case between A and B it is material, and perhaps decisive, that a large number of other persons have committed the same tort against the defendant as the plaintiff. It is an odd reason indeed to excuse the plaintiff from the consequences that otherwise attach to his actions, given our general premise that the rights of and against third parties should not control the equities between the parties to the immediate suit. And it leaves open the question why a use that cannot create a right of way for an indefinite length of time can create it in a single case. Finally, it is not clear how the frequency of the case bears upon the degree of risk, material to the law of negligence. It is possible for the defendant to argue, at least where the condition caused no previous accidents, that the constant use of the path without harm proves that there was no need for him to take precautions.[19]

The position of the Restatement is further complicated when the defendant harms an infant who has entered upon his land. Under the Restatement, the infant is entitled to the protection accorded to all trespassers under the general exceptions to the no-duty-to-trespassers rules. The Restatement recognizes, however, an additional exception to the general rule which operates only in their favor.[20] This exception keeps the requirement of the artificial condition created or maintained on the property though it need

---

[19]See, *e.g.,* Bottum's Adm. v. Hawks, 84 Vt. 370, 79 Atl. 858 (1911). There the defendant maintained an open bulkhead that connected with an underground conduit. The bulkhead was not set off from its immediate surroundings, save only for the ten-inch boards around it. The bulkhead was on private property, near a public street frequented by children who attended the public and private schools nearby, all of the above being known to the defendant. When the infant fell into the bulkhead, he was carried off into the conduit and drowned. The argument in favor of liability under these circumstances must be that the defendant was in the best position to avoid the loss in question. But there are two problems that stand between the plaintiff and his verdict even if this test is applied. First, the officials of the two sets of schools, or the infant's guardian, could have done something to remedy the situation. Second, the risk of harm might not have been that great given that the area near the bulkhead had been used with great frequency by children with no report of any prior accident that could have prompted corrective action. The opinion in *Hawks,* though much criticized, does contain an excellent statement of the difficulties with the attractive nuisance doctrine. 84 Vt. at 373–76, 79 Atl. at 860–62.

[20]Restatement of Torts 2d, § 339.

not be created by the defendant. But the references to "constant" trespassers on a "limited area" of the defendant's property are replaced by a different set of requirements designed to take into account the infant's special position. Thus one crucial question is whether the owner has knowledge or means of knowledge that children are likely to trespass in forbidden corners, even though there is no affirmative duty to seek them out.[21] Another is whether they will be exposed to an unreasonable risk of bodily harm or death from the artificial condition, because they will be unable to discover it or realize danger. A further gloss to the exception is that "the utility to the possessor of maintaining the condition and the burden of eliminating the danger [must be] slight as compared with the risk to the children involved."[22]

The rule is odd in most of its particulars. The insistence that the condition be artificial makes no sense where that condition is not created by the defendant or those for whom he is otherwise accountable. The act requirement of the tort law is not designed to extend the defendant's liability to the acts of a stranger, as the Restatement requires here[23] in unexplained contrast to its position on the scope of the defendant's duty to constant trespassers. Again the reference to the infant's appreciation of the risk appears quite unnecessary because the plea of unilateral assumption of risk should be sufficient in its own right even if the trespass of the infant plaintiff is disregarded. Nor is it quite clear why the duty is limited to cases where the defendant knows or has reason to know that infants may be present, because it seems quite consistent with the general law of negligence to impose upon the possessor of land in appropriate cases the reasonable costs of search,[24] especially since the Restatement is prepared to bend the act requirement where a stranger created the condition. Finally, we must question the willingness of the Restatement, within its own premises, to allow the defendant to continue his activities on the ground that the risk to trespassing children is not unreasonable unless "it involves a grave risk to them which could be obviated without any serious interference with the possessor's

[21]*Id.* at § 339, comment g.
[22]*Id.* at § 339(d).
[23]*Id.* at § 339, comment d.
[24]Fowler V. Harper & Fleming James, Jr., *supra* chap. VII, note 2, at 1458-59.

legitimate use of his land.''[25] The balance of equities between the parties is at sharp variance with the general law of negligence, where the plaintiff need show only that the precautions are cost justified.[26] And in an odd sense it conflicts with the premises of a system of strict liability. Once it is decided, for whatever reason, that the defendant prima facie owes a duty of care to the trespassing child, his self-interest should not be a valid excuse for nonperformance, any more than it is in other contexts.

The complex form of the rules governing trespassing children is in essence an attempt to reconcile the "public interest in the possessor's free use of his own land for his own purposes"[27] with the general theory of the law of negligence, and thus to give a partial, though imperfect, vindication to the place of private property recognized in a system of strict liability. But the compromise must fail. Where negligence is the basis of the tort law, there is little or no place for special immunities based upon the possession of land. Yet after the theory of negligence is rejected in its general form as a basis for liability, then it is difficult to see why it should act as a dominant constraint in the special context of infant trespassers. Instead the narrow point for decision should be whether the plaintiff's infancy constitutes a sufficient reason to override the plea that the plaintiff was on the defendant's land when the defendant harmed him. That reply then must be adjudged insufficient, and for the same reasons that infancy states an insufficient defense to the prima facie case based upon causal principles. Again the plaintiff appeals to his own personal weaknesses as a source of legal strength. The infant has a parent or guardian of his own, and he should not be allowed by his own entry to place upon the defendant the affirmative obligations of guardianship. If it is an important social goal to protect children, the costs of protection should be borne socially by paying owners of property sufficient funds to take the necessary precautions now required by the law of torts, or indeed by paying the damages from social funds. The costs of the protection will be borne by the public who benefits, and they will be made explicit so that it will

---

[25]Restatement of Torts 2d, § 339, comment n.

[26]Fowler V. Harper & Fleming James, Jr., *supra* chap. VII, note 2, at 1458.

[27]Restatement of Torts 2d, § 339, comment n.

be possible in a social context to determine whether they are justified by the benefits they provide.

The special rule for infant trespassers cannot be justified, moreover, by saying that it is too costly for the guardian to "follow him around with a keeper, or chain him to the bedpost."[28] Even if courts paid attention to problems of cost, they are nowhere taken into account by the complex of rules that govern the legal position of the infant trespasser. While there must be some cases where the costs of prevention are less for occupiers of land than for guardians, as perhaps in the turntable cases, there is no reason to expect that to be true in the general case.[29] Small infants must be watched constantly to protect them from all sorts of hazards for which there will be no recovery under the law of tort regardless of the rules for infant trespassers. In these cases the duty of care rests in express terms upon the infant's guardian. Once that duty is recognized, then it is by no means clear that the additional costs he must incur in order to protect the child are in general greater than those the law now imposes upon the landowner to achieve that same end, particularly since we do not know on whose land the accident will take place, the number of infants to be protected, or the set of precautions appropriate to the range of possible cases.[30] Indeed, if the costs of case-by-case determinations were so high that the duty of care had to be assigned to either the guardian or occupier of land alone, most likely the duty is better placed upon the guardian, while if those administrative constraints are ignored the appropriate response is to make the complex analysis on a case-by-case basis, dealing with all the complexities of coordination raised by the *Carroll Towing* formula as best we can, to see which party had the better opportunity to avoid the harm. Yet this sort of inquiry too is ruled out by the infant-trespassers rules, for they nowhere make reference to the costs of prevention by guardians. Where, moreover, their role has been considered, the strong, indeed overwhelming, run of cases has held that it is "harsh" to bar the child's recovery by imputing to it the guard-

---

[28]William L. Prosser, *supra* note 14, at 427, 429 (1959).

[29]But see Richard A. Posner, *supra* chap. V, note 3, at 59. "It is cheaper for land occupiers to fence the occasional structure or piece of equipment presenting this special hazard than for parents to pen their children."

[30]Holgate v. Bleazard, [1917] 1 K.B. 443.

ian's negligence.[31] Efficiency is not the explanation for the rules on infant trespassers as they now stand, nor is it the tool that will aid in their coherent reformulation.

Even if the doubtful efficiency point is conceded, however, it still remains the case that questions of cost should not control the legal issue. The argument that it is too costly for an infant to protect itself, or for a guardian to protect him, in the end only raises anew the plea of private necessity. Concede that the costs are too great, and no sufficient reason appears to impose upon strangers affirmative obligations designed to relieve infants or guardians from the cost of their burdens. The discussion of the good Samaritan rule makes it clear that there is insufficient reason to create liability because the defendant can avoid the harm with but "little" inconvenience to himself. If the costs of preventing the harms are too great for the potential plaintiffs to bear, then they must bear the harms when they occur.

The plea that the defendant has entered upon the plaintiff's land does not, of course, state an absolute defense, for it admits of exceptions by way of reply for the very reasons that a defendant can urge to override the prima facie case for trespass to real property. Of greatest practical importance is the reply that A gave B permission to enter upon his land.[32] Thus A's permission to enter could serve as an affirmative defense to justify an entrance that otherwise would be a trespass. Likewise, in an action by B to recover for harm caused by A, B could plead the permission as a sufficient reply to A's defense based upon B's entrance. The issue of permission is fundamental, then, because in both contexts it shows that consensual arrangements can displace the general rules of tort and property and that the common law distinction between trespassers and visitors, be they licensees or invitees,[33] is crucial as

---

[31]Fowler V. Harper & Fleming James, Jr., *supra* chap. VII, note 2, at § 23.3; William L. Prosser, *supra* chap. VI, note 1, at 490.

[32]To note yet another plea, consider the sequence: (1) B hit A, (2) A entered B's land, (3) B compelled A to enter B's land. Here the issue of compulsion is raised as a reply. Note that if C compelled A to enter the land, A has an action against C. But the plea is not a good reply in the action between A and B.

[33]The distinction between licensees and invitees is not that crucial. It has been abolished, for example, by statute in England, Occupiers' Liability Act (5 & 6 Eliz. 2, Ch. 31, 1957). The distinction between trespassers and visitors still remains of theoretical importance.

a matter of legal theory even if it has been called into question in recent years.[34]

The permission to enter land can be either express or implied. Where the permission is given expressly, there is normally little problem except in cases where the defendant seeks to show by way of rejoinder that it was obtained in an improper fashion, say by duress or misrepresentation. Where permission to enter is implied from all of the circumstances, it is more difficult, but by no means impossible, to establish it. Doubtless there is permission to enter a shop in order to transact business there, or to use a path to the door of a private house in order to speak to its residents. Most likely there is permission to use wide stretches of unoccupied beach, where the license to enter could be inferred from the custom of the area, at least if no signs are posted to the contrary.[35] The category of implied permission is thus crucial to the tort law, but it is also one easily abused. The most important instance of its misuse arises in connection with the doctrine of "allurements" or "attractive nuisances," whereby virtually any kind of "plaything" is said to either allure or attract, and hence "invite" a child to use the land.[36] While it is possible, though difficult, to conceive of cases where the "attraction" could amount to an invitation, the general rule must be that it does not, lest every pool, porch, car, or tree convert an infant from a trespasser into guest.[37] While it has been said that a child (again no mention is made of the guardian question) will "follow a bait as mechanically as a fish,"[38] it seems doubtful in the extreme that the attraction should do the work of external compulsion, and thereby excuse as a matter of course the infant's entrance onto the defendant's land. Indeed the modern tendency has rightly been to minimize the importance of the refinements of "allurement" and "attractive nuisance" and to deal, one way or the other, with the question of the

---

[34]Rowland v. Christian, 69 Cal. 2d 108, 70 Cal. Rptr. 97, 443 P.2d 561 (1968).

[35]McKee v. Gratz, 260 U.S. 127 (1922).

[36]See Bottum's Adm. v. Hawks, 84 Vt. 370, 386, 79 Atl. 858, 865 (1911), on the possibilities of abuses; see Harrison v. City of Chicago, 308 Ill. App. 263, 31 N.E.2d 359 (1941), as an instance of that abuse.

[37]Fowler V. Harper & Fleming James, Jr., *supra* chap. VII, note 2, at 1454–55.

[38]*Id.* at 1455.

infant's trespass without resort to fictional notions of implied invitation.[39]

The case is not necessarily closed even where the plaintiff has entered the land with the permission of the defendant. It is quite possible that the permission to enter was conditioned upon the acceptance by the visitor of the risk of harm caused by the defendant, thus raising again the plea of consensual assumption of risk. It would be nice to have an express agreement that spoke to the conditions attached to entry, but in almost all cases the plaintiff's permission to enter is given and received with no thought as to its legal consequences in the event of injury. The best that can be hoped for in the absence of the direct evidence is some approximation to the allocation generally thought fair for the different contexts in which the entry is made. Essentially, the problem involves the proper implication of terms in a contract where the parties have not spoken about a matter crucial for the resolution of their differences.

The difficult problem, and one that admits of no definitive solution, is to match the distribution of risks with the circumstances under which the permission for entry was granted. There is, of course, no necessary relationship between the two, because the external circumstances of entrance are being used only as evidence of the agreement or, more likely, as an unhappy substitute for it. When notice is posted, or warnings otherwise given, they are properly given great weight because they do provide hard evidence of the terms on which entry is allowed.[40] But where none is present other techniques must be resorted to. One possible ap-

---

[39]The allurement requirement could defeat recovery in cases like United Zinc & Chemical Co. v. Britt, 258 U.S. 268 (1922), where the youths killed by the dangerous conditions on the defendant's land were not attracted to it by them. The decision—clearly correct in my view—by Justice Holmes is consistent with his position while on the Supreme Judicial Court of Massachusetts. See, *e.g.,* Holbrook v. Aldrich, 168 Mass. 15, 16, 46 N.E. 115 (1897): ("Temptation is not always invitation . . . [I]t does not excuse a trespass because there is a temptation to commit it, or hold property owners bound to contemplate the infraction of property rights because the temptation to untrained minds to infringe them might have been foreseen.") Holmes' opinion in *Britt* has been approved in England. See Mourton v. Poulter, [1930] 2 K.B. 183, 191; Frederick Pollock, Law of Torts 406 (15th ed. 1951).

[40]See generally Fowler V. Harper & Fleming James, Jr., *supra* chap. VII, note 2, at § 27.13, for a discussion of the effect of warnings.

proach is to apportion the risk as a rough function of the benefits to each party that result from the plaintiff's entry upon the defendant's land.[41] Suppose entry is allowed for the plaintiff's exclusive benefit, that he might gather without charge firewood for his own use. In the absence of evidence to the contrary, he takes the risk of all accidents, save perhaps those caused by concealed dangerous conditions known to the defendant of which the plaintiff was ignorant.[42] Yet if the plaintiff enters for the defendant's exclusive benefit, the defendant could well be required to bear the risks of all accidents he caused just as if the entry had never taken place. Finally, in the common case where both parties derive some benefit from the plaintiff's entry onto the land, the permission could be treated as subject to the condition that the plaintiff takes the risk only of those harms that could not be avoided by the exercise of reasonable care by the defendant.[43]

This scheme is subject to the obvious objection that the categories are not distinct; a little ingenuity could place almost all cases in the middle category, particularly if indirect benefits to either party are taken into account. It also conflicts with the traditional line drawn at common law between invitees and licensees. Both invitees and licensees usually enter the defendant's premises

---

[41]That is the kind of test used to determine the duty of care presumptively placed upon a bailee. For the basic classification, see Coggs v. Bernard, 2 Ld. Raymond 909 (1703). It is also the explanation for the willful and wanton standard found in automobile guest statutes. See generally William L. Prosser, *supra* chap. VI, note 1, at § 34.

[42]Restatement of Torts 2d, § 343a.

[43]In effect this last rule returns us to a common law negligence standard by way of reply. Thus the pleas proceed: (1) defendant hurt the plaintiff; (2) plaintiff assumed the risk by (implied) agreement; (3) the risk so assumed did not extend to those cases in which the defendant could have saved the plaintiff from injury if he had taken the appropriate steps to make the premises safe. This sequence of pleas is required in principle only if the acts of the defendant are regarded as a necessary prerequisite for recovery. It should not be necessary where (as is generally the case) the protection of licensees and invitees is required even where the hazards are not of the defendant's own creation. With the act requirement to one side, the plaintiff could reach the ultimate issue in a prima facie case that alleges that the defendant did not keep his promise to take reasonable steps to keep the premises safe, steps which could have spared the plaintiff injury. No matter which form is adopted, the agreement provides the source of the duty of care in cases of accidents to visitors. By way of contrast there is no satisfactory account (moral or economic) of the duty concept in cases of accidents between strangers. The duty requirement is necessary to negligence theory to get around the good Samaritan problem, for only it explains why someone should do what he is able to.

for the mutual benefit of the parties, but the allocation of risk will be quite different in the two cases.[44]

There are thus at least three possible ways to assign the risk of accidents when the plaintiff enters the defendant's land as his visitor. We could seek to match the risks of accidents with the benefits that each expects to derive from the visit; we could draw the common law distinctions between licensees and invitees; and we could decide that any categorization of visitors is apt to produce more complications than it is worth. There is here very little of principle at stake in the choice, for none of these possible solutions could pretend to be correct most of the time. Whichever is selected can at best act only as a surrogate for the express agreement that could settle the matter once and for all.

[44]The licensee is said to enter the land subject to the dangers its condition holds for the occupier; the only duty on the occupier is to disclose to the visitor concealed dangers of which he has knowledge. Restatement of Torts 2d, § 342. On the other hand, the occupier owes his business invitee a duty to take reasonable steps to see that the premises are safe, a standard that can be easily converted into one that requires the premises to be safe. See, *e.g.,* Rose v. Melody Lane of Wilshire, 39 Cal. 2d 481, 247 P.2d 335 (1952), where the court held that the jury was entitled to find for the plaintiff after he had fallen from a defective bar stool. Even though the defect could not have been discovered by reasonable inspection, the jury was entitled to find that the defendant should have taken precautions against that possibility by adding some kind of support to the chair. It is another case where *res ipsa loquitur* converts the law of the case from negligence to strict liability.

X. Conclusion

Now that we have completed an examination of the most common pleas of a system of strict liability, it is, I believe, profitable to attempt a brief overview of the system. As a theoretical matter, the systems of strict liability and negligence begin from opposite points of view. The basic question with a system of strict liability always takes the form, is it fair to let one party gain an advantage at the expense of the other, and includes in the system all pleas that are designed to eliminate the benefits that are so obtained. The negligence system tends to ignore the relationship between the parties and asks only of each taken in isolation, is there any reason to believe that he should not have acted as he did, where the harm that ensues is itself never taken as that reason. To answer the questions posed by it, the law of strict liability creates a prima facie case that rests on causal notions alone, subject to a series of defenses, replies, and the like, which are designed to reduce the gap between notions of causation and those of responsibility. On the other hand, the law of negligence tries to state many of the necessary qualifications upon the causal principle by adding the element of "reasonableness" to the prima facie case. These two distinct methods of qualifying causal principles work to create a convergence between the two systems, but, even so, it is quite clear that the two systems will yield different results in certain contexts, as the treatment of the defenses of infancy, insanity, compulsion, and best efforts clearly reveals.

There are, however, a large number of situations where the particular responses of the negligence system are inconsistent with its basic premises, but which follow as a matter of course from a theory of strict liability. Thus the negligence rules of "but for" causation and proximate cause do not on their face appear either to permit or to require an account of intervening causal occurrences; yet the negligence law has always made those inquiries, and in terms not very dissimilar from those required by the strict causal paradigms. In a similar vein, there is nothing about the negligence law that requires the recognition of the division between trespass and case. Yet that division, central to a scheme of strict liability, dominated the law for a long period of its history and still retains its theoretical and practical importance today. Again, the special problems of the good Samaritan and the general acceptance of the maxim, you take your victim as you find him, are but consequences of the general causal requirement of a system of strict liability. They remain central to the tort law today, even though they mesh only with difficulty with the general law of negligence. So too the defense of assumption of risk is accommodated into the tort law, even in the face of persistent arguments that seek to make it, with all of its qualifications, part of the comprehensive defense of contributory negligence. Finally, the response of the law to the case of plaintiff's trespass, however confused it may be in itself, shows as well that the straight negligence principles are hedged in by limitations that have nothing whatsoever to do with the conduct of the reasonable man.

Even if the comparisons with negligence law are put to one side, this system of strict liability, despite its attractions as a system of corrective justice, might be criticized on the ground that it is not worth the social costs that it imposes, costs measured by its inefficiency compared to other systems that might be offered as substitutes for it. It is very difficult to estimate a claim of this sort in the best of circumstances (for what is the price of justice?) and almost impossible to do so where no bill has been, or is likely to be, presented. Nonetheless a few general remarks can be offered.

First, there are at least two sets of tools, traffic laws and eminent domain powers, that can be used to promote social efficiency in a manner that does not offend any principles of corrective justice. Second, the use of the defense of assumption of risk permits the parties to reduce inefficiencies by appropriate contractual means. Third, there are a large number of cases in which the choice between the two theories will not change the incentives under which the parties act, but which will only determine whether or not recovery is appropriate in the given case. Finally, the costs created by the explicit introduction of cost-benefit arguments into the legal rules may themselves exceed the benefits that they are intended to confer.

Once these arguments are put to one side, we are left only with those cases of accidents between private parties who owe no affirmative obligations to each other, but who might have wished to assume such obligations if there were not legal or practical barriers to the transactions that might create them. In these cases, the economic approach asks us in at least some cases to abandon our views on the initial assignment of property rights, on the ground that the aggregate costs of accidents (together with the costs of prevention) will be reduced by the substitution of new rights in their place. But here technical problems suggest that it is impossible to operate a system that can seize in practice the theoretical benefits promised by the economic approach. At this point the question of costs and benefits should perhaps be restated: What possible benefits from the rearrangement could outweigh the costs of a compulsory reassignment of property rights?

As against the economic theories, the similarities between the common law of negligence and the system of strict liability developed here are perhaps more important than the differences between them. Both treat the tort law as a system not of resource allocation but of corrective justice. These similarities suggest, as historically has doubtless been the case, that the bulk of cases will be decided in the same way, more or less elegantly perhaps, regardless of the substantive position adopted. It is quite easy for juries and indeed for lawyers to treat "fault" first as an equivalent for negligence and then as an equivalent for responsibility, and thus bridge the gap between the two systems with but a single ambiguous term. That indeed is what is done whenever we say that the traffic laws provide us with the standard for decision in negligence cases. Hence the choice between these two systems comes down to the few, but still important, cases where the outcome will rest upon choice of theory. With respect to those cases, I hope that I have shown that the system of strict liability better enables us to sort out the claims of corrective justice and thus to fashion a coherent set of rules out of the building blocks of common understanding that should lie at the heart of any system of tortious responsibility.

RECOMMENDED READING

Barnett, Randy E., and Hagel, John, eds. *Assessing the Criminal: Restitution, Retribution, and the Legal Process.* Philadelphia: Ballinger, 1977.

Becker, Gary S. "Crime and Punishment: An Economic Approach." *Journal of Political Economy* 76 (March 1968):169–217.

Bird, Otto A. *The Ideal of Justice.* New York: Praeger, 1967.

Borgo, John. "Causal Paradigms in Tort Law." *Journal of Legal Studies* 8 (June 1979):419–55.

Buchanan, James M. *Cost and Choice.* Chicago: Markham, 1969.

———, and Thirlby, G. F., eds. *L.S.E. Essays on Cost.* London: Weidenfeld and Nicolson, 1973.

Cheung, Steven N. S. "Transaction Costs, Risk Aversion, and the Choice of Contractual Arrangements." *Journal of Law and Economics* 12 (April 1969):23–42.

———. "The Structure of a Contract and the Theory of a Non-exclusive Resource." *Journal of Law and Economics* 13 (April 1970):49–70.

———. "The Fable of the Bees: An Economic Investigation." *Journal of Law and Economics* 16 (April 1973):11–33.

———. *The Myth of Social Cost: A Critique of Welfare Economics and the Implications for Public Policy.* London: Institute of Economic Affairs, 1978.

Coase, Ronald H. "The Problem of Social Cost." *Journal of Law and Economics* 3 (October 1960):1–44.

Demsetz, Harold. "The Exchange and Enforcement of Property Rights." *Journal of Law and Economics* 7 (October 1964):11–26.

———. "Some Aspects of Property Rights." *Journal of Law and Economics* 9 (October 1966):61–70.

137

———. "Toward a Theory of Property Rights." *American Economic Review* 57 (May 1967):347–59.

———. "When Does the Rule of Liability Matter?" *Journal of Legal Studies* 1 (January 1972):13–28.

———. "Wealth Distribution and the Ownership of Rights." *Journal of Legal Studies* 1 (June 1972):223–32.

Donisthorpe, Wordsworth. *Law in a Free State,* pp. 132–158. London: Macmillan, 1895.

Dworkin, Ronald. *Taking Rights Seriously.* Cambridge: Harvard University Press, 1977.

Epstein, Richard A. "Pleadings and Presumptions." *University of Chicago Law Review* 40 (Spring 1973):556–82.

———. "Intentional Harms." *Journal of Legal Studies* 4 (June 1975): 391–442.

———. "Causation and Corrective Justice: A Reply to Two Critics." *Journal of Legal Studies* 8 (June 1979):477–504.

———. "Nuisance Law: Corrective Justice and Its Utilitarian Constraints." *Journal of Legal Studies* 8 (January 1979):49–102.

Evers, Williamson M. "Toward a Reformulation of the Law of Contracts." *Journal of Libertarian Studies* 1 (Winter 1977):3–13.

Fletcher, George P. "Fairness and Utility in Tort Theory." *Harvard Law Review* 85 (January 1972):537–73.

Furubotn, Eirik, and Svetozar, Pejovich. "Property Rights and Economic Theory: A Survey of Recent Literature." *Journal of Economic Literature* 10 (December 1972):1137–62.

Gordon, H. Scott. "The Economic Theory of a Common-Property Resource: The Fishery." *Journal of Political Economy* 62 (February 1954):124–42.

Hall, Jerome. "Criminal Attempt—A Study of Foundations of Criminal Liability." *Yale Law Journal* 49 (March 1940):789–840.

———. "Interrelationships of Criminal Law and Torts." *Columbia Law Review* 43 (September 1943):760–75.

Hamowy, Ronald. "Freedom and the Rule of Law in F. A. Hayek." *Il Politico* 36 (1971):349–77.

Hayek, Friedrich A. *The Constitution of Liberty.* Chicago: University of Chicago Press, 1960.

————. *Studies in Philosophy, Politics, and Economics.* Chicago: University of Chicago Press, 1967.

————. *Individualism and Economic Order.* Chicago: Gateway, 1972.

————. *Law, Legislation, and Liberty,* 3 vols. Chicago: University of Chicago Press, 1973, 1979, forthcoming.

————. *New Studies in Philosophy, Politics, Economics, and the History of Ideas.* Chicago: University of Chicago Press, 1978.

Hogskin, Thomas. *Natural and Artificial Rights to Property Contrasted.* Clifton, N.J.: Kelley, 1973.

Hudson, Joe, and Galaway, Burt, eds. *Considering the Victim: Readings in Restitution and Victim Compensation.* Springfield, Ill.: Charles C. Thomas, 1975.

————. *Restitution in Criminal Justice: A Critical Assessment of Sanctions.* Lexington, Mass.: Heath, 1977.

Kirzner, Israel M. *Competition and Entrepreneurship.* Chicago: University of Chicago Press, 1973.

————. *Perception, Opportunity and Profit.* Chicago: University of Chicago Press, 1979.

Landes, William M., and Posner, Richard A. "Salvors, Finders, Good Samaritans, and Other Rescuers: An Economic Study of Law and Altruism." *Journal of Legal Studies* 7 (January 1978):83-128.

Laster, Richard E. "Criminal Restitution: A Survey of Its Past History and an Analysis of Its Present Usefulness." *University of Rochester Law Review* 5 (Fall 1970):71-80.

Leoni, Bruno. *Freedom and the Law.* Los Angeles: Nash, 1972.

Lewis, C. S. "The Humanitarian Theory of Punishment." *Res Judicatae* 6 (June 1953):224-30.

Machan, Tibor. *Human Rights and Human Liberties: A Radical Reconsideration of the American Political Tradition.* Chicago: Nelson-Hall, 1975.

Mack, Eric. "Egoism and Rights." *The Personalist* 54 (Winter 1973): 5-33.

————. "Natural and Contractual Rights." *Ethics* 87 (January 1977): 153-59.

————. "Egoism and Rights Revisited." *The Personalist* 58 (Summer 1977):282-88.

————. "Liberty and Justice." In *Justice and Economic Distribution,* ed. J. Arthur and W. Shaw. Englewood Cliffs, N.J.: Prentice-Hall, 1978.

Mueller, Gerhard O. W. "Compensation for Victims of Crime: Thought Before Action." *Minnesota Law Review* 50 (1965–66):213–21.

Nozick, Robert. *Anarchy, State, and Utopia.* New York: Basic Books, 1974.

Passerin d'Entrèves, A. *Natural Law: An Introduction to Legal Philosophy.* London and New York: Hutchinson's University Library, 1951.

Posner, Richard A. "A Theory of Negligence." *Journal of Legal Studies* 1 (June 1972):29–96.

————. "Epstein's Tort Theory: A Critique." *Journal of Legal Studies* 8 (June 1979):457–75.

Rizzo, Mario J. "The Cost of Crime to Victims: An Empirical Analysis." *Journal of Legal Studies* 8 (January 1979):177–205.

————, ed. *Time, Uncertainty, and Disequilibrium: Exploration of Austrian Themes.* Lexington, Mass.: Heath, 1979.

Rothbard, Murray N. *For a New Liberty: The Libertarian Manifesto,* rev. ed. New York: Macmillan, 1978.

————. "Justice and Property Rights." In *Property in a Humane Economy,* ed. Samuel L. Blumenfeld. La Salle, Ill.: Open Court, 1974.

Schafer, Stephen. *Compensation and Restitution to Victims of Crime,* 2d ed. Montclair, N.J.: Patterson Smith, 1970.

Spencer, Herbert. "Prison-Ethics." In *Essays, Scientific, Political, and Speculative,* vol. 3. New York: Appleton, 1892.

————. *The Principles of Ethics,* 2 vols. Indianapolis: Liberty Classics, 1978.

————. *Social Statics.* Clifton, N.J.: Kelley, 1969.

Weinreb, Lloyd L. *Criminal Law.* Mineola, N.Y.: Foundation Press, 1969.

————. *Denial of Justice.* New York: Free Press, 1977.

ABOUT THE AUTHOR

Richard A. Epstein received his B.A. from Columbia University in 1964, and law degrees from Oxford University in 1966 and Yale University in 1968. From 1968 to 1973 he was an Assistant and Associate Professor at the University of Southern California Law Center. In 1973 he accepted an appointment as Professor of Law at the University of Chicago, after visiting there for the 1972–73 academic year. During the 1977–78 year he was a Fellow at the Center for Advanced Studies in the Behavioral Sciences, and during the summer of 1979 he was a Visiting Fellow at the Max Planck Institute for Comparative and International Private Law in Hamburg.

Professor Epstein is the author of the third edition of Gregory, Kalven & Epstein, *Cases and Materials in Tort Law* (1977), and has published extensively on legal topics, especially on tort law, in the *American Bar Foundation Research Journal, The Journal of Legal Studies, The University of Chicago Law Review, The Stanford Law Review,* and other legal periodicals. His book, *Products Liability, Its Past and Present,* is scheduled to be published in 1980.